How to Apply for the MEXT Scholarship

Book 1 of Mastering the MEXT Scholarship:
The TranSenz Guide

Travis Senzaki

For You,

You, with the big ideas and dreams;
You, who will change the world;
You, who just need a signpost to point you to the path to
success.

INTRODUCTION

Hello and congratulations on your decision to apply for the Japanese Government Monbukagakusho (MEXT) Scholarship for research students!

My name is Travis and I will be your guide through this application process. I spent three years working on MEXT scholarship applications at a large, private university in Japan and handled over 500 applications for the Embassy and University Recommendation application processes – only about 10% were successful. Since then, I have helped thousands of MEXT scholarship applicants through my blog.

I want to leverage that experience to help you, whether you just heard about the MEXT scholarship for the first time yesterday, or whether you are applying for the second or third time. No matter where you are in the application process, I am confident that I can offer experience and advice that will give you an advantage over other applicants. This application is a zero-sum game. There are only a certain number of slots to go around, and you need to be better than the competition to secure the scholarship you deserve.

Please do not let that frighten you. As I said, **you deserve this scholarship.** And you can earn it.

I am excited to be with you here on your journey.

Travis Senzaki
Akita, Japan
http://www.transenzjapan.com/blog/

What This Book Will Do For You

This book will explain the Japanese government Monbukagakusho (MEXT) scholarship, outline the application procedure, and help you develop the mindset and specific application strategy to succeed. It is based on seven years of experience working with thousands of applicants to bring you the most comprehensive information possible.

This is the first book in my series of guides on the MEXT scholarship for research students (which means "graduate students"). It is also the most important book, in my opinion, regardless of where you are in your application journey.

Over the last several years, I have helped thousands of applicants apply for the scholarship through my blog, but the articles there focus on individual parts of the application process. This guide will take you start-to-finish through the application process. This book and series takes the best of my articles, plus additional research and exercises, to walk you through the process step-by-step.

With this series of guides, you can pick up wherever you are in the application process, find tips and experience from past applicants as well as my research, and follow through to the end. But, regardless of where you are, I encourage you not to skip the chapters on the Application Strategy later in this book. If you get the mindset and strategy down, then even if you do not read the rest of the books in the series, you will have the most important tools you need to find the information through other sources. (The other books will be a shortcut for you, though!)

In this first book, I will introduce the scholarship, explain the mindset you need to succeed, help you figure out if you are eligible to apply, and help you create your application strategy that will distinguish you from other applicants and maximize your chances to earn the scholarship.

In the first chapter, we will cover the basics: the scholarship categories, the different ways to apply, and the scholarship benefits. I will explain how to get started with each kind of application process, and the pros and cons of applying for the Embassy Recommendation scholarship and the University Recommendation scholarship.

Next, we will cover perhaps the most important fundamental subject in this entire series: Your application mindset. In chapter two, I will help you understand how you need to approach the scholarship, including the mistakes many applicants make that eliminate them from contention, and the habits you can adopt to stand out as a professional, desirable applicant.

In the third chapter, we will review your eligibility. I will explain the eligibility criteria in detail, including the eligibility criteria that are not released in English. The most challenging eligibility criteria to understand is the GPA requirement, since MEXT uses a 3-point scale that is not used anywhere else in the world (including by Japanese universities). I will help you convert your grades to that scale.

Once we have covered the basics of applying and determined that you are eligible, in the fourth and final chapter, we will create your application strategy. Even if you get nothing else out of this book, or any of the other books in the series, that chapter will set you on your path to success.

Other books in this series (some available for pre-order at select retailers now) will cover:

1. How to Apply for the MEXT Scholarship: This book! http://www.transenzjapan.com/mms1/

2. How to Write a Scholarship-Winning Field of Study and Research Program Plan: How to write your field of study and research program plan
   - Mastering the most important document in your application package.
   - http://www.transenzjapan.com/mms2/
3. How to Find your best Degree Program and Adviser for the MEXT Scholarship: How to research universities in Japan and contact potential advisers
   - Figuring out where you want to study, who you want to study under, and making the first steps to establish a connection.
   - http://www.transenzjapan.com/mms3/
4. MEXT Scholarship: The Embassy Recommendation Application Process: Screenings, interviews, letters of acceptance, and placement
   - Everything you need to know about the Embassy application process, from submitting your documents through placement at a university.
   - http://www.transenzjapan.com/mms4/
5. MEXT Scholarship: The University Recommendation Application Process: Screenings, interviews, and selection
   - Everything you need to know about applying for the scholarship through a university in Japan.
   - http://www.transenzjapan.com/mms5/
6. Preparing to Move to Japan: A Handbook for MEXT Scholarship Winners: Once you've been selected, what's next?
   - How to arrange your visa and travel, what to pack, and other preparation for your studies in Japan
   - http://www.transenzjapan.com/mms6/
7. MEXT Scholar and Beyond: Life in Japan: Living in Japan as a MEXT scholar
   - Scholarship-specific information, including the language program, extending your scholarship, and losing it.

- General information about life in Japan: Housing, banks, phones, bringing your family, and more!
- http://www.transenzjapan.com/mms7/

What You Need to Do

I will share everything I know about the MEXT scholarship process and best practices for the application, but let's get this out of the way first:

You are going to have to do the work.

There is no substitute for hard work and research in this application process. I do not teach cheap gimmicks or ways to cheat the system (I am not aware of any). I teach a systematic way to strengthen your application and increase your appeal to the professors and government staff who will review your application. But it is up to you to put those steps into practice.

You do not necessarily need to do *everything* I describe in this book or the rest of the series, so don't panic. Each step you choose to implement improves your chances and each step you ignore gives your competition the chance to pass you by. It is up to you to decide how much you really want this scholarship and how hard you are going to work.

Still with me? Good!

Academic Support

There are a few other assets you need to bring, starting with your academic background. There is nothing I (or even you, most likely) can do about your grades in your last degree. The higher they are, the better your chances will be. If they are below the mark that we discuss in the chapter on eligibility, then you cannot even apply. So, grades are on you.

If you are the kind of person who is willing to invest in yourself by buying a scholarship application guidebook, I assume you are also the kind of person who invested in themselves by earning excellent grades.

You will also want to have access to an expert in your academic field, such as your adviser from your last degree. I am an expert in the application process, I cannot help you evaluate your particular research topic or give advice specific to your field. If I could do all of that, for every field out there, I would be out there winning Nobel prizes instead of writing this book.

Finally, if you are not a native English speaker, you will want to find one among your friends who can help review your application later on. I can do reviews for a fee, but I cannot possibly hope to individually serve everyone who reads this book. There is only one of me and 24 hours in a day.

Aside from the willingness to put in hard work, you will not need any of the things above to begin, so while you are assembling your team of experts, let's get started!

DOWNLOAD ALL OF THE EXERCISES, LINKS, AND RESOURCES IN ADVANCE

I have created a bonus document to go with this book that you can download in advace. It includes all of the links that appear in the book, so you can simply click them instead of having to type them out.

Each chapter also has an accompanying series of exercises that will help you work through the contents as you go along. While the questions are listed in the book, the download pack contains them in worksheet form, so you can fill in the answers as you go along. Writing your thoughts on paper is much more powerful than keeping them in your head, so I highly recommend that you complete them as you go.

http://www.transenzjapan.com/bonusmms1/

Along with those worksheets, I will also send you the TranSenz GPA Spreadsheet from Chapter 3. Plus, when you sign up for the mailing list, I will send you updates to the contents of this book or the bonus materials as the scholarship process changes or I learn more from other applicants' experiences.

DEFINITIONS AND TERMINOLOGY

MEXT:

The Japanese Ministry of Education, Culture, Sports, Science and Technology. If you put all of those letters together, you get MECSST, which is pronounced "MEXT".

You may also see the ministry called *Monbukagakusho* or *Monbusho*. The first is the official Japanese name and the second is the old Japanese name that still persists, especially among former scholarship winners. All mean the same thing.

JASSO:

The Japan Student Services Organization. JASSO is an quasi-governmental "Independent Administrative Institution" that supports MEXT's efforts. They are charged with providing information about education in Japan in English and Japanese and also administer payment of government scholarships, including the MEXT Scholarship, on behalf of MEXT.

Research Student (*kenkyūsei*):

When MEXT refers to the scholarship for "research students", they mean *kenkyūsei*. The better translation is "graduate student" and this term refers to all graduate-level students, whether enrolled in a degree-seeking program, or not.

In Japanese, each individual graduate school within a university is called a *kenkyūka*, or research division. *Kenkyū* literally means research, but this term is translated as "graduate school" in almost all situations. For some reason *kenkyūsei*, which is derived from "student enrolled in a *kenkyūka*" is translated as "research student".

Translated terms in Japan are inconsistent like that.

Research Student (*hiseikisei*):

Universities use the term "research student" to refer to a student who is affiliated with a graduate school, but is not enrolled in a degree program. As you can see, the word in Japanese is different, despite being translated into English with the same term as *kenkyūsei. Hiseikisei* means non-regular student and can refer to pre-graduate students who have not yet been admitted to the degree program or short-term students who have no intention of seeking a degree but just want to take courses and conduct research.

Many MEXT scholarship winners, especially those who are selected through the Embassy Recommendation, start their studies in Japan as *hiseikisei* research students.

Degree-Seeking Student:

A degree-seeking student is a student who has passed the entrance exam and been matriculated into the degree program, as opposed to a *hiseikisei*. You can be a degree-seeking student at any level (undergraduate, Master's, or Doctoral). Once you are a degree-seeking student, you are "on the clock" to complete your degree within the designated standard number of years of enrollment: four for undergraduates, two for Master's degrees, and three for Doctoral degrees.

MEXT scholars who cannot complete their degrees within the designated standard years will lose the scholarship as soon as it becomes clear that they are unable to complete on time.

Master's Degree:

For this book, I will use the term Master's degree to encompass all Master's level degrees, whether academic or not. In Japan, degrees like Master of Arts or Master of Science are considered to be academic degrees. There are also Master's-level professional degrees (see below) that fall under this category, such as MBAs and professional Master's in teaching, etc.

Doctoral Degree:

For this book, I will use the term Doctoral degree to encompass all doctorate level degrees, whether academic or not.

5-year Doctoral Degree:

Some programs in Japan offer a 5-year Doctoral degree program with no Master's degree awarded in the interim. For the sake of the MEXT scholarship, you would still be considered a Master's level student for the first two years, even though you would not earn a degree after that point, and would have to apply for a scholarship extension to cover your participation in the final three years, which would be considered a Doctoral degree, from MEXT's point of view.

If you have a Master's degree already, it may be possible to enter a 5-year Doctoral Degree from the third year of studies.

Professional Degree:

Professional degrees are degrees that are required for a specific job qualification, rather than "pure" academic degrees. Examples include MBA, MD, MDDS, DVS, JD, DBA, etc. There is no prejudice against professional degrees within the evaluation system, but like anything else, you would have to justify why it is the most appropriate degree for your goal.

Embassy Recommendation:

The process of applying for the MEXT scholarship by submitting your application to the Japanese embassy or consulate in your home country. In this process, you will still need to contact universities later for Letters of Acceptance.

For more on the Embassy Recommendation process, please see Chapter 1: Understanding the MEXT Scholarship.

University Recommendation:

The process of applying for the MEXT scholarship by submitting your application to the university in Japan that you wish to attend. In this process, you do not need to go through the Japanese embassy, except for your visa, after acceptance.

For more on the University Recommendation process, please see Chapter 1: Understanding the MEXT Scholarship.

Priority Graduate Program:

This is a subset of the University Recommendation. There are some university programs that are pre-approved by MEXT to be able to nominate a specific number of students each year for the scholarship with the guarantee that all will receive it, if eligible. Typically, these programs have very narrow eligibility requirements, for example, they may be limited to students with a particular nationality, in a specific degree program and level, and studying in a specific language. While the list of PGP programs is sometimes made available, the eligibility criteria for each one is often not revealed. If you meet the eligibility criteria for one of these programs, then your competition level is much lower and your chances of winning the scholarship skyrocket, but it is almost impossible to know in advance.

Primary Screening:

The initial round of the application screening conducted at the embassy/consulate or university. This is the competitive round and determines who will be recommended to MEXT for the scholarship. If you pass the Primary Screening and are recommended to MEXT, you are practically guaranteed to receive the scholarship, so that is what we will focus on.

Secondary Screening:

MEXT's screening of recommended candidates. Although this screening takes longer than the Primary Screening, it is not competitive and it is practically unheard of for an applicant to lose the scholarship at this point. MEXT is just double-checking the embassy or university's work to make sure you are eligible.

Placement Preference Form:

One of the application documents that exists only in the Embassy Recommendation application process. This is where you list your top three universities where you would like to enroll as well as your target academic adviser at each one. I cover the process of searching for universities and professors in more detail in Book 3 of this series: *How to Find Your Degree Program and Adviser for the MEXT Scholarship* http://www.transenzjapan.com/mms3/

Field of Study and Research Program Plan:

The most important application document under your control. This is where you explain what you want to research in Japan and why. It is so important that Book 2 of this series, *How to Write a Scholarship-Winning Field of Study and Research Program Plan*, is entirely dedicated to that one form. http://www.transenzjapan.com/mms2/

Certificate of Graduation:

This does *not* necessarily mean your diploma! A Certificate of Graduation is any official document from your university stating that you have met all of the requirements and completed your degree program, along with the date.

Certificate of Expected Graduation:

This is an official letter from your university stating when you are expected to complete your degree and graduate. It does not need to guarantee that you *will* graduate on that date (no university would guarantee that, because you still have to pass your classes). It is the university's guarantee that you *can* meet all of your requirements and graduate on that date. In other words, they are only saying that it is not impossible for you to graduate on the given date.

If you have not yet graduated by the time you submit your application, then you need to provide this document in place of a Certificate of Graduation.

Certificate of Grades:

This can also be called an academic transcript, certificate of marks, record of performance, etc. It is the document that shows your academic performance in each class you have taken at your current university.

Explanation of Grading System:

This is a scale that shows what the various grades "mean" and their relative value. See Appendix A for examples of different kinds of grading systems.

Graduation Thesis:

This is the culminating paper or project for your degree. You will be asked to submit an abstract of your thesis for the screening process. Especially at the undergraduate level, not all degree programs have a final thesis. That is fine. If you do not have a thesis or final project, check with the Embassy or University for guidance. You may be asked to submit an abstract of a term paper related to your research or told that you do not need to submit anything.

Since the requirement is to submit an abstract, not the whole thesis, you do not need to have written the thesis yet.

Visa:

Japan uses the word "visa" differently most other countries. In Japan, a visa is only permission to enter the country. Once you arrive in Japan and pass through immigration, you have used up your visa and no longer have one (except in the case of multiple-entry visas). Instead, you will have a Residence Status, which is your permission to stay in the country.

MEXT scholarship winners have a special student visa application process that bypasses the usual requirement to obtain a Certificate of Eligibility. You will receive more information about the process and specific instructions after selection, but you will only be able to obtain your student visa at the Japanese embassy or consulate in your home country that serves your place of residence.

Residence Status:

Once you pass through immigration in Japan, your visa becomes invalid and you receive a residence status, instead. Your residence status is your legal permission to live in Japan to pursue the activities listed in that status. MEXT scholarship winners will have a Student Residence Status.

It is possible to change your residence status while living in Japan. For example, after graduating, you could apply to change your status to a working status. However, you cannot change your residence status during your MEXT scholarship award period or you will lose the scholarship.

CONTENTS

INTRODUCTION
Downloadable Exercise Worksheets and Resources
Definitions and Terminology
CHAPTER ONE: Understanding the MEXT Scholarship
What is the MEXT Scholarship for Research Students
Categories of the MEXT Scholarship for Research Students
Application Process Overview
Embassy Recommendation
University Recommendation
Applying to Both
Domestic Selection
Exercise 1: Determining Your Approach
CHAPTER TWO: Successful Applicant Mindset
Be Confident
Be Professional
Don't Be Cocky
Exercise 2: Mindset
CHAPTER THREE: Eligibility
Academic Background and Degree Completion
Basic Eligibility Criteria: Measurable
Basic Eligibility Criteria: Unmeasurable
Disqualification Criteria
Field of Study
Past or Present Residence in Japan
GPA
Embassy-Imposed Additional Requirements
Exercise 3: Eligibility

CHAPTER FOUR: Your Application Strategy
Your Theme: How You Will Serve
Going from Theme to Goal
Validating and Revising Your Goal Ideas
Crafting Your Goals
"MEXTifying" Your Goal
Think About Your "Opposition"
What Will Help and Hurt Your Chances
Exercise 4: Your Application Strategy
IN CLOSING
About the Author
All Exercises
APPENDIX A: GPA CONVERSION CHARTS
Grading Systems with Examples and Conversion Charts
Sample Calculations
APPENDIX B: PRIORITY COUNTRIES
APPENDIX C: REFERENCES AND RESOURCES

CHAPTER ONE:
Understanding the MEXT
Scholarship

WHAT IS THE MEXT SCHOLARSHIP FOR RESEARCH STUDENTS?

The MEXT scholarship is a scholarship program offered by the Japanese Ministry of Education, Culture, Sports, Science and Technology (MEXT) for international students who want to come to Japan to study. The scholarship is available at various levels, from a one-year undergraduate study abroad program all the way up through graduate degrees.

This book and series focuses on the application for the graduate-level scholarship.

Benefits of the Scholarship

As of the time of publication, the MEXT scholarship offers:

- Complete tuition exemption for the duration of your studies;
- A stipend of 143,000 - 145,000 yen/month, depending on your degree level, plus a cost of living adjustment in some areas of 2,000 - 3,000 yen/month;
- One free round-trip international flight ticket between your home country and Japan, to bring you here for the start of your studies and get you home after you are finished; and
- Payment of all entrance exam and matriculation fees.

You can even extend your scholarship award period. If you start as a Master's level research student, then matriculate to a Master's program and finally continue on to a PhD, it is possible to extend the scholarship each time you move up to cover your entire duration of study. All told, that could be over 10 million yen in scholarship stipend payments, and that's not even counting the value of the tuition and flight tickets.

That's a pretty generous offer by any standard. The stipend is enough to live on. I have even seen students with families cover the cost of living for their spouse and children under their stipend, in more rural areas.

Purpose of the Scholarship

Of course, the Japanese government is not just being altruistic here. This is not a handout or even a need-based scholarship. It is an investment on their part. They have specific goals established for you as a graduate of the program.

Specifically, the program is designed to:

- Educate future leaders in politics and education from other countries, to instill in them an understanding of and sympathy toward Japan, that they will retain as they advance through their careers;
- Educate students who will return home and become ambassadors for their Japanese universities, contributing to recruiting more students, including self-financed students, to study in Japan in the future;
- Deliver an economic boost to Japan, both through the direct benefits to the economy of having international students in the country and also through training future leaders in business who will retain connections with Japan throughout their career;
- Develop ambassadors for Japanese culture who will spread interest in the country once they return home; etc.

According to follow-up reports, the goals of training leaders in politics and education has had the strongest results in Asia and especially ASEAN, where a Japanese education offers an advantage over many domestic programs and graduate degrees are relatively rare. MEXT graduates in the past have quickly risen to senior government posts and leadership within local universities.

In developed countries, particularly in North America, Western Europe, and Oceania, the goal of developing Japanese cultural ambassadors has yielded stronger results, because of the relative strength of local educational institutions.

Keep these outcomes in mind as you go through your scholarship application. You will want to take every opportunity to indicate to the scholarship reviewers that you have the clear potential to deliver the value they seek on their investment.

Scholarship Availability

The MEXT Scholarship for Research Students is the largest category of scholarships offered by MEXT, but that does not necessarily mean that the opportunities are plentiful.

As of 2015, the last year for which MEXT has published its scholarship data, the scholarship for Research Students was available to applicants from 168 countries and there were a total of 4,042 scholarship slots available per year. The number of scholarships has not gone up. It may seem like a large number at face value, but when you break it down by how the slots are allotted, it starts to look small very quickly.

As of May 1, 2017, there were a total of 188,384 International students enrolled in higher education in Japan. 46,373 were in graduate school and 9,166 were MEXT Scholarship recipients, at all levels. Compared to the previous year, that is an increase of 17,000 students, including 3,000 graduate students, but a decrease of 300 MEXT Scholarship winners. The competition is only getting fiercer.

Although there are around 4,000 slots available, you are competing for one of a much smaller number.

The scholarship is divided into two primary application

processes: the Embassy Recommendation and University Recommendation applications, which we will cover in more detail later on. Slots are further divided among individual countries or embassies for the Embassy Recommendation application and among universities in Japan for the University Recommendation. You might find yourself competing for only 2 slots allotted to the consulate that serves your region (as in the US for the Embassy Recommendation) or a half dozen slots allotted to the university where you want to study (for the University Recommendation).

What I am saying is that you should expect fierce competition and take every step in your power to give yourself and advantage over other applicants. That is exactly what we will be doing for the remainder of this book and series.

Other Types of MEXT Scholarships

I mentioned earlier that there are other types of MEXT scholarships that are not covered by this book. While these scholarships are not relevant to you, I am going to list them out here because you may come across the terms in other searching (and in the application form itself), so it is important to know what you can ignore.

- **Undergraduate Students:**
  For high school students between 17-24 years of age as of April 1 in the year they start their scholarships, who want to complete their Bachelor's degree in Japan. This scholarship also includes a year of Japanese language studies before the degree starts, and students will then be placed in a Japanese-taught degree program at MEXT's discretion. As of 2015 (the last year for which data is available), there were 460 slots open to applicants from a total of 100 countries. The only application method is Embassy Recommendation.

- **Colleges of Technology:**
  In Japan, Colleges of Technology are a separate category of higher education institution from universities. They award a three-year technical degree that is not equivalent to a Bachelor's degree. High school students from 40 developing countries are eligible to compete for what was 86 total slots in 2015. Like the undergraduate program, this scholarship includes a year of Japanese language preparation before students take their programs entirely in Japanese. The only application method is via the Japanese Embassy.

- **Japanese Studies Scholarship:**
  This is a one-year scholarship program for undergraduate exchange students who will be spending a year in Japan as part of a degree program taught at a university in another country. As the name suggests, it only applies to students majoring in Japanese studies (Japanese language and culture). Students from 74 countries were eligible for a total of 190 slots, as of 2015. It is only available at a predetermined list of universities in Japan. It is possible to apply via the Japanese Embassy or via one of the designated universities in Japan.

- **Teacher's Training:**
  This is the only other graduate-level MEXT scholarship program. The scholarship duration is for up to one-and-a-half years of special training in a teacher's training program and may include six months of Japanese language training, if necessary. There were only 89 slots available to applicants from 64 countries, as of 2015.

Compared to these scholarship opportunities, the MEXT Scholarship for Research Students has significantly more spaces available - 4,042 as of 2015, is open to applicants from more countries, and is frankly much more valuable. Graduate education, when you are most specialized in your discipline, gives you the best opportunity to make the most of the resources available to you in Japan.

CATEGORIES OF THE MEXT SCHOLARSHIP FOR RESEARCH STUDENTS

Although this is called the MEXT Scholarship for "Research Students", remember from the definitions in the Introduction, *you can apply for a degree program through this scholarship.*

Now, let's break down what it means to be a research student, Master's degree student, or Doctoral students under the MEXT scholarship.

Research Student

Everyone who earns the scholarship is a *kenkyūsei* "research student" in the sense that they are a graduate-level student. However, you can also be enrolled as a *hiseikisei* "research student" at a university.

In this sense, research student means "non-degree" student. In most cases, this is a student who is affiliated with a particular Master's or Doctoral program, but has not yet passed the entrance exam to start their degree. Many MEXT scholars start as research students for a semester, or up to two full years, depending in some cases on their academic ability and in some cases on the policy of the university.

Applicants for the Embassy Recommendation MEXT scholarship often spend their first semester in Japan in an intensive Japanese language program to help teach some basics for everyday life. Students in this program are also research students.

You may also start as a research student if your university does not permit you to take the entrance exam before arriving in Japan or if you arrive in the wrong semester to start the degree. Some degree programs will only matriculate new students in either the spring or the fall.

The second type of research student, a "pure" research student, is one who is enrolled in a graduate degree program overseas and only plans to come to Japan to conduct their field research, with no intention of matriculating to the degree program at a Japanese university. This type of student is practically unheard-of in the MEXT scholarship program.

You can be a research student at either the Master's or Doctoral level, depending on the degree program that you plan to enter.

There is certainly nothing negative about being a research student. In fact, unless you are in a particular rush to finish your degree and return to your home country (for example, if you are on a temporary leave of absence from your job), then it is probably a better idea to spend a semester as a research student if you can. This allows you to get used to the Japanese university system and living in a new country before you go "on the clock" for your degree program.

The only time that you cannot become a research student is if you are repeating a previous degree. For example, if you earned a Master's degree in your home country and wanted to take a second Master's in Japan, you would not be able to start as a Master's-level research student, because that would be an academic step backward. You would have to enter directly into the degree program.

You could, of course, become a Doctoral-level research student and move on to the Doctoral program. And really, why wouldn't you?

Roles of a Research Student

As a research student, your activities are largely up to your academic adviser's discretion. However, you will likely be attending classes and conducting research. You will need to spend a minimum of 10 hours per week in class or active research, as that is a minimum requirement to maintain your student visa. You will have all the rights and privileges of an enrolled student during this time, as well.

While you will not be enrolled in the degree program yet, you should be able to "transfer" credits earned as a research student to count toward your degree after you matriculate.

While you are a research student enrolled in the intensive Japanese language program, you will not be taking classes at the university, but you will likely be meeting regularly with your adviser to plan and start work on your research.

Benefits and Duration as a Research Student

As a research student, your tuition is waived (for national universities) or covered by MEXT (for public or private universities), as with degree-seeking students. Your stipend is 143,000 yen per month, plus a possible 2,000 - 3,000 cost of living adjustment, depending on your location.

You can remain a research student for a maximum of two years, if you start in April, or one-and-a-half years if you start in September/October. That time limit includes the time spent in Japanese language studies, if applicable.

By the end of your time limit as a research student, you must take and pass the entrance exam to the degree program that you want to enroll in and must simultaneously apply to extend your MEXT scholarship. Otherwise, you would have to return home at the end of your research student period.

Degree-Seeking Student

Master's, PhD, and Professional Degree Programs

You can enroll directly in a degree program or start as a research student and extend your studies to include a degree program or two, which is the most common approach, especially under the Embassy Recommendation MEXT scholarship.

There are two degree levels and two special categories of degrees. The levels are, of course, Master's and Doctoral, as explained in the definitions in the Introduction.

One special type of program is professional degrees, such as an MBA (Master of Business Administration), LLM (Master of Laws), JD (Juris Doctorate - law degree), MD (Medical Doctor), etc., which are not standard academic degrees, but are rather career-focused graduate programs. They can be at the Master's or Doctoral level.

The other is a five-year integrated doctorate, which is a Master's and PhD program combined, but does not award an interim Master's degree after the first two years. For scholarship purposes, you would be considered a Master's degree student for the first two years of the five-year program and a PhD student for the final three years. Just like any other student extending from a Master's to PhD program, you would need to apply for a scholarship extension in the middle. You would not automatically be granted a five-year scholarship.

At both the Master's and Doctoral level in Japan, *you will be expected to conduct original research*. There is no such thing as a purely "taught Master's", where you would just attend classes to earn your degree. At the Doctoral level, however, there are programs that are purely research PhDs and others that will require some classes. You will need to research your specific program for more details.

Degree Program Duration

In Japan, you have two years to complete a Master's and three years to complete a Doctoral program. If you do not complete the degree within that time, you would not be able to extend your scholarship. (In fact, as we will cover in detail later on, as soon as it becomes apparent that you cannot complete your degree in that amount of time, you would lose your scholarship immediately.) If you are unsure whether you can complete your degree in that amount of time, that is a great reason to start as a research student, to give yourself a head start on your requirements.

For a program such as an MD, that is typically followed by a residence before you earn the right to practice medicine, you still only get the scholarship to cover the three academic years of the program. You would also need special additional certification to be able to participate in any clinical sessions. MD programs would also require you to be fluent in Japanese.

Benefits of Being a Master's or Doctoral-level Student

Your tuition is waived or paid for by MEXT. The stipend amount is 144,000 yen per month for Master's-level students and 145,000 yen per moth for Doctoral-level students, as of 2018, though it is subject to change. Students at both levels may receive the 2,000 - 3,000 yen per month cost of living adjustment, depending on the university's location.

Which Should You Apply For?

Applicants often ask me whether they have a better chance of success if they apply as a research student or as a degree-seeking student right off the bat. As long as both options are available to you, the answer is that it does not matter.

If you have a choice, my recommendation is to start as a research student. This is more to increase your chances of success *after* you are selected than before.

As we discussed earlier, once you start your degree program, you have a limited amount of time to complete it. But your first semester in Japan is going to be difficult. You will need to adjust to a new culture and a new education system. You will have to set up your housing and get used to daily life. You may even be inviting your family to move to Japan to join you during that semester, which is going to take even more time as you get them settled. Book 7 of this series offers a guide to settling in in Japan, with more information.

Its better to give yourself flexibility to do that while you are not "on the clock" for your degree. You lose nothing by being a research student first.

In some cases, though, you will not have a choice. If you are applying through the University Recommendation, you will find that some programs only accept research students and some only accept degree-seeking students. If you make the wrong selection in those cases, you will show the university that you did not care enough to read the applications guidelines, and that will hurt your chances.

For the University Recommendation, you can only arrive in Japan starting in the fall semester (September or October), but some degree programs only accept new students matriculating in the spring. In that case, you would have to start as a research student. Even if your degree program does accept new students in the fall, you might want to consider starting as a research student, anyway, to give yourself time to adjust before starting the degree program. In that case, though, realize you may have to be a research student for a full year, if you have a program that only matriculates new students in the fall.

If you are applying for the Embassy Recommendation, then you will almost certainly spend your first semester in an intensive Japanese language program, which is also considered research student status. Ultimately, it is up to the university that accepts you whether or not to place you in this program, but if your Japanese ability is below N2 level, then it is probably safe to assume they will want you to take that program. The Japanese language program is designed to get you up to speed for day-to-day Japanese so that you can take care of yourself, your shopping, your banking, your rent, etc. It is not designed to teach you academic Japanese for studying.

Factor that semester in when you are considering when you will arrive in Japan and when you start studies in your actual program. If you want to start your degree program in the fall, then you should either arrive in the spring to take the Japanese language program then matriculate directly to the degree in the fall, or arrive in the fall, take the Japanese language program, then spend a semester as a research student, and start your degree a full year after you arrive in Japan. That's the course of action that I would recommend.

The final thing to consider in your decision is your prospective adviser's opinion. If your adviser wants you to start in a particular semester, listen to their input as well.

Ultimately, remember that your arrival semester has more to do with your success after arrival than it does with your success in the application process.

APPLICATION PROCESS OVERVIEW

Now that we have discussed the different levels of degree that you can apply for, let's go into a little more depth about the two application processes and their differences.

The two application processes are the Embassy Recommendation and University Recommendation. The process you choose is going to have a significant impact on the way you go about your application, from the timing, to the paperwork, to even how many universities you will need to contact.

Perhaps most significantly, it will have an impact on your odds of success.

I will go into more detail on each process, including step-by-step instructions for each form and application document, steps, and specific advice to increase your chances of success in later books in this series. But for now, I will lay out the basics of both to help you choose which one is best for you.

(Hint: In general, I recommend starting with whichever comes first, depending on when you read this. So pay particular attention to the timeline for each.)

EMBASSY RECOMMENDATION

Most MEXT Scholarship winners earn their scholarships by applying through the Japanese embassy or consulate in their home countries. While the process is a little longer and more complex than the University Recommendation, it still offers the greatest chances, especially if you are prepared to face each of them.

In almost all cases, I recommend applying for the Embassy Recommendation first, unless it is simply too late for you to apply as you are reading this. (See the timeline below.)

Let's start by looking at some of the advantages and disadvantages.

Advantages and Disadvantages

For most applicants, the Embassy Recommendation offers

more advantages than disadvantages. Including:

- **Save on test fees:** You do not need to submit TOEFL or JLPT test scores to apply for the Embassy Recommendation if you do not have them. Instead, you will take language proficiency tests at the embassy after you pass the document screening. However, you may need to submit language proficiency test scores later when you apply to universities for a Letter of Acceptance after the Primary Screening.

- **Possibly save on postage fees:** You can apply by submitting your documents by domestic mail or delivery in person (check with the embassy or consulate for specific instructions), so you do not need to pay for expensive international mail services at first. You may need to send your documents by international courier to universities after passing the Primary Screening, but at that point, your scholarship award is practically guaranteed, so the expense does not hurt as much.

- **More slots available:** In almost all cases, you will be competing for a larger number of slots than you would if you applied for the University Recommendation. Notable exceptions to this rule include the US, where the Embassy Recommendation slots are divided up among the consulates, so there are fewer available to each applicant. However, that should also divide your competition into smaller groups!

- **Compete with your countrymen:** If you apply via the Embassy Recommendation, you do not need to worry about differences in the grading system between countries giving particular applicants an advantage.

There are two primary disadvantages to the Embassy Recommendation: Time and interference.

- **Time:** The Embassy Recommendation application process typically starts in May or June of the year *before* you plan to start your studies, so you need to be preparing well in advance - perhaps over a year before you graduate. If you want to start your degree in Japan in April or even October, you should be starting your application no later than April 2018, and probably even earlier, as I will discuss in the timeline below.

- **Local government interference:** Your home country government can impose additional screenings and conditions. For example, it might limit the fields of study available (India divides available slots into sciences and humanities categories; the Philippines has appeared to favor disaster-response engineering in previous years), might impose a pre-screening to determine who is allowed to apply and compel you to return home immediately after graduation (Mexico), or might have local government officials sit in on your interview (Malaysia). This can add complexity to your application process. But on the other hand, if you are prepared for this challenge, you may have an advantage over the applicants who are not.

That last comment is something important to keep in mind, especially as we turn to your mindset in the next chapter. Whenever you are tempted to see something as a disadvantage or challenge, realize that the same challenge applies to all applicants. If you know about it and prepare for it in advance, then it becomes an advantage for you.

Unless, of course, you are competing against the Prime Minister's daughter, or something like that. In that case, there's really nothing you can do. But I sincerely hope that is not the case for you.

Application Timeline

So, when do you need to start your application? At least a year before you plan to start your degree in Japan.

Specific dates will vary by country, so be sure to check with the Japanese embassy or consulate where you plan to apply, but here is a general image of the application timeline. The same timeline holds true whether you plan to arrive for the spring (April) or fall (September/October) semester.

Links to all of the books referenced below can be found in the "About the Author" section at the end.

Year	Month	Step	Notes
2 Years Before Arrival Year	Oct - Dec	Determine your field of study and research question. Start researching and drafting your Field of Study and Research Program Plan	See Book 2 for more details.
1 Year Before Arrival	Jan - Mar	Identify your target universities and prospective advisers in Japan. Finish the first draft of your Field of Study and Research Program plan and start reaching out to professors to establish relationships.	See Book 3 for more details.
	Apr - May	Application guidelines and forms released on MEXT and Embassy websites. Start your application!	See Book 4 for more details.
	May - Jun	Application submission deadline	

Year	Month	Step	Notes
1 Year Before Arrival	Jun - Jul	Document screening, language proficiency tests, embassy interview	See Book 4 for more details.
	Late Jul - early Aug	Results of Primary Screening Released: At this point you can be 99.9% certain of your scholarship results! Start contacting universities for Letters of Acceptance	
	Aug 24	Deadline to contact universities to ask for an LoA.	
	Sep - Oct	Usual deadline to submit LoAs to the Japanese embassy or consulate	
	Oct - Nov	Secondary Screening (a.k.a. The Long Wait, Part I). You may or may not receive a confirmation of passing the Secondary Screening from your embassy.	
	Nov - Dec	University Placement Process (a.k.a. The Long Wait, Part II)	
Year of Arrival	Dec - Jan	Final Results and University Placement released!	See Book 6 for more details.
	Jan - Mar	Spring Semester Arrivals: Visa, travel arrangements, and packing for your trip to Japan!	
	Jul - Sep	Fall Semester Arrivals: Visa, travel arrangements, and packing for your trip to Japan!	

Year	Month	Step	Notes
Year of Arrival	Apr or Sep	Settle in to life in Japan in your degree program or language studies. Establish your day-to-day life and routines. Prepare to extend your scholarship to move on to a degree program, if necessary. Start thinking about inviting your family to join you, if applicable.	See Book 7 for advice and further information.

Don't worry. It looks like there's a lot of work ahead of you, but you do not need to tackle everything at once. The whole purpose of this guide series is to break the process down into simple, smaller steps, to help ease you through the application with minimal stress and confusion!

Document Submission and Screening

The Call for Applications will usually come from the Japanese embassy or consulate in your home country around April. Remember that this is the call for applications for the scholarship starting a full year or more later!

That announcement should include the specific applications procedures for your country, including the application deadlines, as well as all of the forms you need. In later books in this series, I will include sample forms that I have created based on past year's versions, but you should always get the most recent version of the application form from the embassy's website.

To find the website for the nearest Japanese embassy or consulate, refer to the Japanese Ministry of Foreign Affairs web page below:

http://www.transenzjapan.com/embassies/

(To make it easier for you to type, all link references in this book will go through shortened links on my website. The direct links are also available in the bonus document pack.)

Depending on your country, you may have a single embassy, multiple consulates, or no physical Japanese embassy at all. If you have a single embassy, then your process is straightforward, but in the other cases, you are going to need to do a little more work.

If there are multiple Japanese consulates, then it is likely that each one serves only a specific area. You do not get to choose which consulate to apply to. You have to apply to the one that is responsible for the area you live in. Check their websites for further details.

In some cases, there may be no Japanese embassy in your country. This is most often the case in areas that have been hit by war, or countries where there is minimal relations with the local government. In that case, you will still find a link to your country's embassy on the page above, but that Embassy may be located in a different country. For example, the Japanese embassy in Yemen is actually located in Riyadh, Saudi Arabia. Yemeni applicants would have to apply through that embassy.

As long as the Japanese Government formally recognizes your country, there will be an embassy to serve you.

Another important resource is MEXT's own web page for the scholarship:
http://www.transenzjapan.com/officialmext/

While the MEXT page is only available in Japanese, you can still use it as a point of reference to see if there are any changes posted. Once MEXT posts the official scholarship guidelines on that page, they will also be available in English and all the forms will be available, too.

Once you have found the embassy's website and MEXT's page, you will want to make a point of checking them at least once per day until the MEXT scholarship application information is posted (if it is not there already). You can do this by adding those pages to the start-up tabs in your internet browser, so that they automatically load every time you open your internet, or by using a service like VisualPing (see Appendix C) that checks websites for changes and notifies you. I will go into more detail about how to set up both of those checks in the book dedicated to the Embassy Recommendation process, later in this series.

Language Proficiency Tests

If you pass the document screening, you will be invited to the embassy or consulate for the Japanese and English language proficiency tests. In some cases, you may have the interview (see the next section) scheduled on the same day.

You are required to submit the Japanese test, even if you are applying for a program taught in English. If have no Japanese ability, it is fine to turn in a blank test. However, if you do have some ability, you should do your best on this test. It is possible that it will be a factor in determining whether or not you spend your first semester in Japan in the intensive Japanese language program.

Of course, the Japanese test is essential if you are planning to apply to a program taught in Japanese!

For most people reading this book, the English language proficiency test is more critical, even though it is technically optional. It is *not* optional if you are applying to a degree program taught in English. Due to bureaucratic rigidity, you may even be required to take this test if English is your native (and only) language. While I have never taken it myself, I have heard from past native speaker test-takers that it can be deceptively difficult, since it is designed for second-language speakers.

In countries where English is not the primary language, these tests can be used to cull a significant portion of the applicants. In Thailand in 2017, for example, the test was broken down into the written and oral tests and 66% of applicants were eliminated after the written test.

MEXT has made past tests available so that you can practice in advance. Whether you are a native or second language speaker, you should absolutely take advantage of them. The next step, the interviews, is the most time-intensive per applicant, from the Embassy's perspective, so the language tests are their last chance to reduce the number of applicants before that process begins.

You can find old tests at:
http://www.transenzjapan.com/tests/

Interview

Once you complete the language tests, the final stage of the embassy's Primary Screening process is the interview. This may even be held on the same day as the language proficiency tests.

The interview is approximately 20 minutes long, and you will face anywhere from 2-5 interviewers in a panel, in most cases. You will need to be prepared to answer questions about your Field of Study and Research Program Plan, your plans for after graduation, and your knowledge of Japan - from your interests to how you will adapt to life there. The chapter on your application strategy will help you stand out in the interview.

The interview will be held in English, in general, but if you have indicated in your application documents that you have some Japanese ability, you may be asked a few questions in Japanese to test your ability.

You may occasionally face a challenging interviewer, too. One who seems out to get you or seems to be targeting you specifically. Keep in mind that the interviewer is probably behaving the same way toward all applicants. He or she probably thinks it is his or her job to see how you react to stress and is being deliberately antagonistic. Do not let that get you down!

As with the other steps, I will go into significantly more detail, including sample questions, strategies, and preparation, in more detail in the book about the Embassy Recommendation Application Process later in this series.

The interview is effectively your "Final Exam" at the embassy. Passing the interview stage means passing the Primary Screening, which all-but guarantees that you will receive the scholarship.

Requesting Letters of Acceptance

Once you have passed the Primary Screening at the embassy or consulate, you are almost guaranteed to be selected as a scholarship winner, but there is one key step remaining. You have to contact the (up to) three universities and professors on your Placement Preference Form to apply for a Letter of Acceptance. Once you have secured at least one Letter of Acceptance and submitted it to your embassy or consulate, then your application process is complete.

You should begin requesting letters of acceptance immediately after you learn that you have passed the Primary Screening. Ideally, you would have already been in contact with your prospective adviser from much earlier in the application process, but this will be your first opportunity to officially request a Letter of Acceptance

Depending on your country, it could be anywhere from early July to mid-August when you receive your notification of passing the Primary Screening. Regardless of the timing, do not delay in contacting universities. You must contact universities before August 24. You should also consider that August is summer vacation in Japan and it may be harder to get a response from universities quickly.

Your embassy or consulate will tell you the deadline to submit your Letters of Acceptance to them. Once you have turned them in, that is the last part of the process for you. The only thing remaining is a maddening wait for 4-5 months for the final results and your placement.

Secondary Screening

Once you have submitted your Letters of Acceptance to the embassy or consulate, they will forward them, along with the rest of your application materials, to MEXT for the secondary screening.

The Secondary Screening is essentially MEXT just double-checking the embassy's work. They will make sure the embassy did not make any mistakes, that you are not researching something like weapons technology, etc. It is not a competitive screening and I have never heard of an applicant being eliminated at this stage, unless they had failed to obtain a Letter of Acceptance from a university (and even in that situation, some applicants succeeded).

MEXT and the embassy will say that your scholarship is not yet guaranteed at this point and that there is a chance of being eliminated, but that is really them just covering themselves in case of something unforeseen. You do not need to worry about it.

Depending on the policy of the embassy in the country where you applied, they may contact you to let you know that you have passed the secondary screening, or they may wait and not contact you at all until after the final university placement is complete

University Placement

As soon as MEXT determines that your application meets its standards, they will start contacting universities from your Placement Preference Form to ask them formally to accept you as a scholar under the scholarship program.

Typically, MEXT will contact the universities in the priority order that you listed them. However, in some cases, if your top choice is a private or public university, they may choose instead to contact the highest national university on your list first. For MEXT, it costs much less to place you at a national university, where tuition is waived for MEXT scholars, than it does to place you at a private or public university, where MEXT has to pay your tuition on your behalf.

During the placement process, you may hear unofficial results directly from the university. For example, if you are in touch with your prospective adviser, they may let you know that MEXT has asked them to host you, even though they are not technically supposed to tell you. If you are planning to arrive in April, the university might also start contacting you at this point about housing for the spring, even though the formal results have not yet been announced. In either of these cases, even if you do not have the formal results, you can treat these unofficial contacts as true.

Once you get the formal results of the Secondary Screening

and University Placement from your embassy, then all you have left to do is to start packing and preparing for your life in Japan! (I will cover this, too, in a later book, based on advice from past MEXT scholars from around the world.)

EMBASSY: COMPETITION LEVEL

In general, the Embassy Recommendation scholarship competition level is lower than the University Recommendation. It is not *low* by any means - competition is still intense, so you need to be prepared work harder than the other applicants.

Each country has a pre-determined number of slots available, so you are only competing with other applicants from your country. In some cases, where there are multiple consulates across the country, the slots available will be further sub-divided among each of the consulates. There is nothing you can do about this. You have to apply at the consulate that serves the area where you live.

In the University Recommendation application process, by comparison, you are competing against all applicants to that university from all countries for a number of slots that is probably similar to or less than the number available to your country through the Embassy Recommendation. That is why I say the competition for the University Recommendation is slightly higher.

The only time you get a choice in where you apply is if you have multiple nationalities. In that case, you will need to select which country to apply in. Applying in a country identified by Japan as a "priority country" should offer more slots. On the other hand, if you are not currently living in that country, they may be less likely to accept your application. If you are debating which nationality you should apply under, it would be best to contact the embassy in advance to determine if they will accept your application.

You can find a list of priority countries in Appendix B.

Please understand, however, that there is no guarantee that a Priority Country will necessarily have more slots than a non-Priority Country. There are other factors that go into determining the number of slots and that number is not published. Other factors could include population and overall quality of higher education in the country.

Determining the Number of Slots

There is no certain list or calculation method, like there is for the University Recommendation scholarship, but there are some ways you can make a guess.

In some cases, the embassy or consulate might just tell you how many slots they have that year or how many scholarship winners they had the previous year. I have heard from past applicants that they were able to find out that way. However, they will not tell you how many other applicants there are in total.

One method is to check the Japanese embassy or consulate's news articles from a year earlier. Depending on how active their PR office is, they might have held an event for all of the departing MEXT scholars before they traveled to Japan. If they did, and wrote an article about it, they are likely to list the number of scholars that are going.

Keep in mind that you should search for articles in both spring and fall. The numbers reported in fall may also include scholarship-winners through the University Recommendation process.

You can also look for forums, subreddits, or Facebook groups for MEXT scholars. One of the most active forums that I refer to (and comment in) is JREF:

http://www.transenzjapan.com/jref/

From posts in that forum in previous years, here are some of the numbers I have found for the 2018 scholarship application cycle (the most recent cycle, as I write this):

- Brunei: 3
- Cambodia: 22 (Out of over 1,000 applicants)
- Canada: 10 (2 for the Vancouver consulate, 4 each for the Toronto consulate and Montreal embassy)
- Hong Kong: 24
- India: 28
- Jordan: 5
- Malaysia: 24
- Philippines: 25 (including 21 in STEM fields)
- Portugal: 3
- Samoa: 3
- UK: 9
- USA: 1-2 per consulate

Obviously, that's a very short list, and I should give the caveat that I have no verification for any of these numbers other than applicants' reports, but if you dig for further forums in English and your native language, you may be able to find more.

For almost all applicants, even applicants from countries with small numbers of slots, those numbers represent a higher number of available slots, or at least higher percentage chance of earning slots, than the University Recommendation, which we will cover next.

UNIVERSITY RECOMMENDATION

The second major application method for the MEXT Scholarship for Research Students is the University Recommendation.

Instead of applying to the Japanese embassy or consulate in your country, you will apply directly to one university in Japan for admission and recommendation to the scholarship all at once. You will not have to go through the embassy at all, until after your scholarship is determined and it is time to apply for your visa.

The University Recommendation application process starts later in the year than the Embassy Recommendation, so if you have missed the embassy's deadline, then you will most likely start with this process. You can also apply for the University Recommendation if you learn that you have not passed the embassy's Primary Screening.

Like we did with the Embassy Recommendation, let's look at some of the advantages and disadvantages of this process, first.

Overview of Application Process

The University Recommendation process can be more complicated than the Embassy Recommendation, because each university can start its application process differently, according to its needs. Perhaps the hardest part about this process is getting the information specific to the university that you want to apply to.

As a consequence, not all of the advantages and disadvantages below will apply in each case.

Potential advantages include:

- **Fewer steps:** You do not need to clear both the embassy and university, only the latter. That means you only need to appeal to an academic audience with your proposal.
- **Focus on one university:** In the Embassy Recommendation, you choose up to three universities and professors, which is more effort and can lead to uncertainty in where you will study. In the University Recommendation, you will be pursuing a single university and single professor from start to finish, allowing for better focus and efficiency.
- **Shorter application process:** The University Recommendation application process begins several months after the Embassy Recommendation, but the scholarship start time is the same. So you will have fewer months of uncertainty between submitting your application and the final results.
- **No local government interference:** Your local government has no say in who gets the scholarship, so if you are concerned about nepotism, discrimination, or corruption, this process is cleaner.
- **PGP programs:** In addition to the general category slots, you may be eligible for specific "Priority Graduate Programs," which have a dedicated number of slots with narrow restrictions on applicant eligibility. If you meet the eligibility criteria for one of these programs, your chances of winning the scholarship skyrocket! (more information below)

The key disadvantages to the University Recommendation application process are the cost of applying and the lack of consistent application information:

- **Possibly restricted to partners:** Some universities in Japan will only accept applications if they have established a formal partnership with your current university.
- **Application information may be hidden:** Not all

universities make it clear how to apply or if they even accept applications. In some cases, universities may select MEXT scholarship candidates out of their pool of general applicants instead of having a separate application process.

- **Test fees:** Unlike the Embassy Recommendation process, you will be required to submit language proficiency test results from internationally accepted tests like TOEFL or IELTS, so you will have to budget for those. Some universities may also ask you to submit other test results, such as the GRE.
- **Mailing expenses:** You will have to send your application by international courier (such as EMS, DHL, etc.) to universities in Japan. If you have to submit replacement documents or correct errors, there is a chance that you will have to send multiple packages this way.
- **Higher competition:** In almost all cases, you will see a higher competition level for the University Recommendation, since you will be competing against applicants from all countries, not just your own.

It is possible to mitigate, if not eliminate, most of these disadvantages. If you prepare far enough in advance, you will have more time to find the application information you need. You might also have a connection with the university, if you reached out during the Embassy Recommendation application.

For cost, part of my goal in this series of books is to help you get the application right the first time so that you will not need to resend any extra documents by courier. We will also go through the eligibility criteria together in chapter 3 so that you can be certain in advance that you are eligible and not throwing money away on a lost cause.

I cannot eliminate the costs – you will still have to pay for language tests and some postage – but hopefully I can save you money.

General Category and PGP

In the previous section, I referred to "general category" and "priority graduate programs (PGP)." Before we go any further, let's get clear on the differences and what that means to you.

General Category

This encompasses almost all of the MEXT scholarship slots at universities around Japan. Each university has a designated number of general category slots, based on the number of international graduate students enrolled at the university during the previous year. MEXT allots scholarships per university, not per graduate school, so you will be competing with all applicants from all graduate schools for one of the scholarship awards.

We will cover the slot calculation and numbers for some leading universities later in this chapter.

Priority Graduate Programs (PGP)

PGPs are specific degree programs that are pre-selected by MEXT to receive a specific number of scholarship slots each year.

These programs typically have a narrow focus, restricted to one degree level in one graduate school. They might also have other restrictions, such as only being available to applicants from specific nationalities, or only being available to scholars studying in Japanese, but that information might not be publicly available.

Each PGP is selected for a period of three years, so if you are applying in 2018, for example, the programs selected in 2016*, 2017, and 2018 would be valid. (*MEXT did not select any new PGP programs in 2016, this is just for reference).

If you meet the eligibility criteria for one of these programs, your chances of getting the scholarship instantly skyrocket. Instead of competing for a handful of scholarships scattered across the university, you would be competing with a much smaller number of students for scholarships designated for your degree program.

Let me give an example to highlight this: In my final year of processing MEXT scholarship applications, we received over 200 applications for the University Recommendation MEXT scholarship. That year, we had two PGP programs with a total of 15 slots available. Only 16 students met the eligibility requirements for one of those two programs. So, 15 out of those 16 applicants won the scholarship (93.75% success rate). However, only 10 out of the remaining 184 applicants earned a general category scholarship (5.43% success rate).

You can find a list of the 2017 PGP programs (valid for the 2018 and 2019 application cycles) on MEXT's website below: http://www.transenzjapan.com/pgp2017/

Unfortunately, this list will not tell you exactly how many slots each program has or what the restrictions on language, nationality, etc., are, but it will give you a place to start looking. Research each of the individual programs and universities to see if you can find additional information.

At the time of publication, only the 2017 list is available (there were no programs selected in 2015 or 2016), but if you downloaded the worksheets as I suggested in the introduction, I will be sure to contact you when new lists are released, as well!

Typically, you do not need to do anything extra to designate your application for the PGP program. If you apply to the university and you are eligible for PGP, your application would automatically be considered in that pool.

Application Timeline

Just like the Embassy Recommendation, I recommend that you start preparing your application approximately six months before you plan to apply. If you are applying for both, as I recommend below, this timing should work out well for you. The University Recommendation formal application process typically begins around September - November, and six months before that is almost exactly the start time of the Embassy Recommendation application process.

If you apply for the Embassy Recommendation and are not successful in the Primary Screening (or you find out about the Embassy Recommendation application just after the deadline), that is the perfect time to start preparing your University Recommendation application.

The exact application dates are going to vary by university, so be sure you are checking your university's website regularly.

Here is how the application process goes.

Year	Month	Step	Notes
1 Year Before Arrival Year	Apr - May	While preparing your Embassy Recommendation application, determine your field of study and research question. Start researching and drafting your Field of Study and Research Program Plan (you need to submit this to the embassy, anyway)	See Book 2 for more details. *Not a strict deadline.

Year	Month	Step	Notes
1 Year Before Arrival Year	May - Jul	Identify your target universities and prospective advisers in Japan. Finish the first draft of your Field of Study and Research Program plan and start reaching out to professors to establish relationships. (Caution: During this time, many other applicants will be reaching out for Letters of Acceptance for the Embassy Recommendation, you need to be careful in your communication to avoid confusion).	See Book 3 for more details. *Not a strict deadline.
	Aug - Nov	Application guidelines may be released on university websites. In some cases, application guidelines may not be released publicly, so it is important to be in touch with the university. Start your application!	See Book 5 for more details. *This is the first hard deadline!
	Sep - Dec	Application submission deadline is typically during this period, depending on the university.	
	Dec Jan	Application guidelines released on MEXT's website, although it is almost always too late to apply by the time these guidelines are released. Document screening and possible interviews by the university.	

Year	Month	Step	Notes
Year of Arrival	Early Jan	Universities finalize selection of PGP candidates for programs that begin in April, notify candidates, and submit nominations to MEXT. PGP candidates selected for nomination are essentially guaranteed to receive the scholarship, but final results will be released in February.	See Book 5 for more details.
	Jan - Mar	Universities finalize selection of general category candidates and PGP candidates for programs that begin in October, notify candidates, and submit nominations to MEXT.	
	Mar - Jun	Secondary Screening (a.k.a. The Long Wait). MEXT double-checks applications, and makes final confirmation of scholarship awards for all October arrivals.	
	Jun - Aug	MEXT releases final results to universities and universities contact individual applicants. (It is supposed to be in late June, but MEXT is routinely late).	
	Jul - Sep	Visa, travel arrangements, and packing for your trip to Japan! (February - March for April arrivals)	See Book 6 for more details.

Year	Month	Step	Notes
Year of Arrival	Apr or Sep	Settle in to life in Japan in your degree program or language studies. Establish your day-to-day life and routines. Prepare to extend your scholarship to move on to a degree program, if necessary. Start thinking about inviting your family to join you, if applicable.	See Book 7 for advice and further information.

Document Submission and Screening

As I mentioned in the "disadvantages" section earlier, each university has its own application process and it is not always possible to predict how and when they will call for applications.

Once you determined the university you want to apply to, you should research that university in detail and start trying to connect with your desired adviser (not as a MEXT applicant at first, but as a student who is genuinely interested in the professor's research – I will cover contacting universities and professors in Book 3 of this series.) That is the best way to ensure that you will get the application information you need.

In some cases, universities will only accept applications from students from partner universities, so they will not send out a public call for applications. They will only reach out through their partnerships.

In other cases, universities might not have a separate application process for MEXT scholars. They could simply select the top candidates each year from their regular, fee-paying applicants. The disadvantage for you in that case is that you would have to pay an application fee. If you get selected for the scholarship, you would get that fee back (universities are not allowed to charge application fees to MEXT scholarship applicants), but if you are not selected, you would lose that money.

Of course, you could choose to see that as an advantage, too: It will limit the number of applications and therefore the competition.

Even in cases where universities have an open call for applications, the dates can vary significantly. Some schools will close the application deadline in August. Others might not start accepting applications until November.

It is essential that you research your target university in advance!

Researching Your University

Unlike the Embassy Recommendation application process, you are only allowed to apply to one university per year through this method, so that limits the number of universities you have to follow up with.

The most effective and efficient way to research your target university is through a partnership with your current university. If there is a partnership in place and you can identify a faculty or staff member at your current university that has a connection to the Japanese university, you can inquire through them.

If that is not an option, you will have to comb through the Japanese university's website. Look through their news archive to see if they posted an announcement in the previous year to say when MEXT applications were open. Check their admissions pages, particularly the scholarship page for international graduate applicants, if one exists. That is most often where you will find the guidelines. You may even be able to find the previous year's application forms, which will give you an idea of what you need to submit even before they update the page.

Application Forms and Guidelines

You need to get the forms and guidelines from the university, since they can vary.

As you saw in the application timeline earlier, most universities accept applications *before* MEXT releases the official forms for the next year. Because of that time gap, some universities use their own forms or modifications of the forms and ask successful applicants to complete the proper MEXT forms later. You need to be sure that you are following the directions for your university.

I send a sample version of the application form to all new members of my mailing list as a thank-you gift, but I deliberately do not provide blank application forms for exactly that reason.

The guidelines for your university will also tell you when and how to submit your application, so even if the forms are all identical, you will need to read that document, anyway.

Once you have completed the forms and submitted them, be prepared for a long wait as the university screens applications.

Interviews

MEXT asks all universities to conduct interviews of applicants during the selection process. These interviews may be in person (unlikely) or conducted by email or Skype. In most cases, the interview will come after an initial cut is made based on the documents. If you get an interview request, it is a good sign, but not necessarily a guarantee, yet.

Unlike the Embassy Recommendation application process interviews, the university is going to be more heavily focused on the academic side of your goals.

While you will not have to deal so much with bureaucrats and general questions, you will probably face more intense academic screening because the reviewer will be an expert in your field.

You will need to be prepared to discuss your Field of Study and Research Program Plan in detail and also answer general knowledge questions about your academic field to establish that you are prepared for a graduate degree.

I will cover the interview and past students' experiences in the book dedicated to the University Recommendation Application Process.

Nomination and MEXT Screening

Once the university has finished its review, they will reach out to let successful candidates know that they have been selected for nomination to MEXT.

At this point, you are permitted to party! Every applicant I have ever heard of who was nominated by the university for the scholarship ended up receiving it, whether they were in the general category or PGP.

Most universities should also contact waiting list candidates and unsuccessful candidates, as well.

If you are a waiting list candidate, the only way to get elevated to full candidate is if one of the selected nominees withdraws before the deadline for universities to submit their nominations to MEXT. Unfortunately, that is very unlikely. Almost every time I have had a nominee withdraw, it was after the deadline, so it was too late for us to recommend an alternate.

If you are one of the unsuccessful candidates, do not take it too hard. The chances are good that no more than one applicant per field of study earned nomination for the scholarship. You could have been the second-best candidate in all of science and engineering, out of dozens of applicants from all over the world, and still miss out. In that case, you would be better served by trying again for the Embassy Recommendation application process, which will start a few months after the university's nomination results.

MEXT Secondary Screening

As with the Embassy Recommendation, this is not a competitive process. MEXT is primarily concerned with double-checking your eligibility, ensuring that you have not applied and been recommended by two different universities, and also checking its own budget.

Japanese universities should all be experienced in this application process, so there is no reason to think that there would be a problem with your eligibility after the university's screening.

If you have applied to and been nominated for multiple universities, MEXT will flag that and will disqualify you. It may also choose to disqualify every other applicant from all of the universities that recommended you. If, for some reason, you find that you have been nominated by multiple universities, you will need to be sure to contact all but one of them to withdraw *before* they send your name to MEXT.

Finally, the Japanese fiscal year ends in March, between when universities nominate candidates to MEXT and when MEXT makes its final decision. If there is a budget crisis and MEXT's budget is slashed, there is a chance that they could choose to award fewer scholarships. However, this possibility is almost non-existent, so it is nothing to worry about.

University: Competition Level

In general, competition is going to be higher for the University Recommendation application process. Of course, if you qualify for one of the PGP programs that would not be the case!

Unlike the Embassy Recommendation, it is possible to estimate the number of places available at each university. The number of scholarship slots is based on the number of international graduate students enrolled at that university each year, modified by the increase or decrease in self-funded international graduate students from the previous year.

MEXT releases a chart every year that shows how many places are available based on the number of enrolled international students. I have included the chart for the 2018 cycle, below, but keep in mind that this can change year to year. The chart is released along with the University Recommendation application guidelines and forms. As we covered above, this comes after most universities' application deadlines, so the best you can do is refer to the previous year's figures for an estimate.

JASSO also conducts an annual mandatory survey of universities to find out how many international students they have enrolled and publishes that information on its website, so it is possible to get an idea of which universities in Japan have the highest number of international students enrolled, and therefore have the most scholarship slots.

However, JASSO's numbers are for all international students, and MEXT only counts international graduate students, so that means there is an extra step: Once you identify the universities on JASSO's list with the greatest number of international students, you have to go the universities websites to find out from the data they share how many of those students are graduate students.

It's a lot of work. That's the bad news. The good news is that I have already done it for you.

The table below shows the raw number of MEXT scholarship slots that correspond to the number of international students enrolled, based on MEXT's table for 2018. I have also added the names of top universities that fall into that category, based on data released by JASSO and the universities themselves. The universities in this table are the ones that have admitted the highest number of international students overall. So, a university that does not appear in this list is likely to have only 1 to 2 raw slots available.

There are a few ways that this raw number can be modified, which I will discuss below.

Unofficial slot breakdown by university for the 2018 cycle

(estimated based on available reporting by the university and JASSO)

Number of International Graduate Students Enrolled	Number of MEXT Scholarship Slots	Universities in the Category
1001+	9	University of Tokyo, Waseda, Tohoku University, University of Tsukuba, Osaka University, Kyushu University, Kyoto University, Hokkaido University, Nagoya University*, Tokyo Institute of Technology, Hiroshima University
801 - 1000	8	Kobe University
601 - 800	7	Ritsumeikan University, Keio, Chiba University
501 - 600	6	Sophia University
401 - 500	5	Meiji University, Yokohama National University, Kansai University
301 - 400	4	Doshisha University, Josai International University
201 - 300	3	Takushoku University, Hosei University
101 - 200	2	Ritsumeikan APU, Chuo University
0 - 100	1	Japan University of Economics, Osaka Sangyo University

*Reporting was not sufficiently detailed for this university, but this is my best guess based on data available.

Modifying the Raw Figure

There are three ways the numbers above are modified:

1. If a university had zero MEXT scholarship nominees in the previous year, then the maximum number of raw nominees is 1.

2. The raw figure is multiplied by the percent change in self-financed (i.e. not MEXT scholarship) international graduate students from the previous year.
    So, for calculating 2018 slots, each university would multiply its raw number by the number of self-financed international students enrolled in 2017 divided by the number of self-financed international students enrolled in 2016, rounding the result to the nearest whole number. Using this calculation, Kyoto University, for example, saw a significant enough increase in self-financed international graduate student enrollment in 2017 to earn an additional slot, as confirmed by a faculty member there.

3. Each university may recommend two additional scholars if the university is willing to cover the scholars' transportation expenses to Japan.

Priority Countries and Slots

MEXT has a list of priority countries (see Appendix B) and requires that 75% of each university's nominees for each program come from those countries. If your country is not on the list, then the competition level is going to be much higher.

A university that has 8 general scholarship slots can nominate no more than 2 students from non-priority countries. A university with 4-7 general scholarship slots can nominate only 1. A university with fewer than 4 scholarship slots is not able to nominate any students from non-priority countries.

So, if your country is not on the priority countries list in

Appendix B, you must select your university from the 21 universities in the chart above that have four or more general category slots.

Dividing Slots Among Graduate Schools

Keep in mind that the numbers we calculated above are for each university, as a whole. In almost all cases, universities are going to divide the slots among their graduate schools in advance. (Much like how, in the Embassy Recommendation, slots may be pre-divided among individual consulates).

Most universities find it difficult or impossible to compare the quality of an applicant in Science and Engineering to an applicant in Sociology. The reviewers would be different, their expectations would be different, and there would be no objective basis for comparison. Dividing slots ahead of time makes for reduced conflict.

The number of MEXT scholarship slots available probably will not divide evenly into the number of graduate schools. In some cases, there will not even be enough slots for each graduate school to get one. Each university will have its own approach to dividing slots, but keep in mind that the end result is that there will likely be only 1-2 slots available in your field of study.

Top Global University Project Universities and Extra Slots

Universities selected for MEXT's "Top Global University Project" (also called the "Super Global University Project" in some cases) have additional MEXT Scholarship slots available. These slots are technically considered to be "Domestic Selection" category scholarships, though they are sometimes awarded together with University Recommendation slots.

See the section on Domestic Selection below for more details.

Rise to the Competition!

Do not let the competition level discourage you. Let it be motivation. You need to be the best applicant and you can be, if you are willing to put in the effort. Throughout the rest of this book and series, I am going to share every bit of advice I have from seven years to improve your chances.

APPLYING TO BOTH: EMBASSY AND UNIVERSITY

Technically, you are only allowed to apply to one form of the application at a time. But because of the way the application timelines work, you *can* apply to both application processes sequentially, if you have to.

Applying for the Embassy Recommendation First

For the Embassy Recommendation, you need to submit your application documents in late May or early June. By the end of July, you should know the results of the Primary Screening, which is essentially the same as the final results.

If you pass the Primary Screening, then you know that you are practically guaranteed to receive the scholarship, so there is no reason to worry about applying for the University Recommendation. If for some reason, you were to not pass the Secondary Screening, it would most likely be because of a problem of such significant magnitude that it would prevent you from ever receiving the MEXT scholarship (for example, a record of being deported from Japan in the past).

If you do not pass the Primary Screening, then you would be out of the application process and still have time to start your application that year for the University Recommendation before it starts between August - December (depending on the university).

In that case, you would not be breaking any rules. Plus, since you would have started your field of study and research program plan, as well as started contacting universities, you would have an advantage over other applicants.

Applying for the University Recommendation First

If you apply for the University Recommendation, you will know between January to March whether or not you have been selected for nomination to MEXT for the scholarship. Just like with the Embassy Recommendation, being nominated is practically a guarantee of earning the scholarship. So, in that case, there would be no need for you to apply to the embassy. Instead, you should be focused on preparing to move to Japan.

If you do not pass the university's screening and receive their nomination, then you still have plenty of time to prepare for the Embassy Recommendation application process that will begin in May or June, for the next year.

If you have got your heart set on the MEXT scholarship and you have no intention of giving up, you can continue this cycle for years. I have known applicants who earned the scholarship in their second and third years applying. Each time you go through the process, refine your Field of Study and Research Program Plan, and practice the interviews, you become a stronger candidate.

Of course, our goal with these books is to give you the advantage of past applicants' experience so that you can earn the scholarship in your first attempt.

DOMESTIC SELECTION

Besides the Embassy Recommendation and University Recommendation, there is a third path to the MEXT scholarship: Domestic Selection.

While the Embassy and University Recommendation scholarships are determined before you arrive in Japan, the Domestic Selection process is typically for applicants who are already enrolled in a Japanese university, or scheduled to be enrolled, as self-financed (non-scholarship) students.

In recent years, due to budget reduction, MEXT has cut back the Domestic Selection scholarship. It is now only available to universities that were selected for the Top Global University Project. Even those universities are only able to nominate new candidates if one of their existing scholarship awardees graduates. See below for more information on Top Global University slots.

Because the slots are so limited and availability is unpredictable, I would recommend that you do not rely on this scholarship approach.

If you do, though, know that the to earn the Domestic Selection MEXT Scholarship, you would essentially have to be the single best international student enrolled at the university, based on the university's own general scholarship application process. Since that process and the criteria differ from university to university, it is impossible to give any advice that will be certain to make a difference. However, if you follow the guidelines we cover in this series, especially about presenting your research, then that should give you an advantage!

Scholarship Benefits: Difference

Domestic Selection scholars do not receive coverage for travel expenses to Japan. This scholarship application process assumes that you are already in Japan or that you are already scheduled to travel to Japan on your own to enroll in a university.

Top Global University Slots

Universities selected by MEXT for the Top Global University project (2014 - 2024) have additional MEXT scholarship slots available through the Domestic Selection scheme.

Type A universities from the chart below are able to host up to an additional 20 MEXT scholars under this scheme and Type B universities can host up to an additional 10 MEXT scholars. This number represents that total number of scholarships available at any time, not the number of new slots each year. Universities can only award a new scholarship if a previous awardee graduates or loses the scholarship, so it is impossible to tell how many will be available in any given year, unless the university announces it.

Some universities may choose to award the scholarship on a year-by-year basis under this scheme and some may choose to award it for the duration of the degree. To find out what your preferred university does, I recommend you check the guidelines on their website.

As with the Domestic Selection scholarship in general, I do not recommend that you deliberately aim for these slots, as they are inconsistent and unpredictable. However, if you are applying to one of the universities below through the University Recommendation process, know that you may also be a candidate for one of the Top Global University Scholarships.

Type A Universities: 20 Slots/Year	
Hiroshima University	Hokkaido University
Keio University	Kyoto University
Kyushu University	Nagoya University

Type A Universities: 20 Slots/Year	
Osaka University	Tohoku University
Tokyo Institute of Technology	Tokyo Medical and Dental University
University of Tokyo, The	University of Tsukuba
Waseda University	
Type B Universities: 10 Slots/Year	
Akita International University	Chiba University
Hosei University	Kanazawa University
International Christian University	International University of Japan
Kumamoto University	Kwansei Gakuin University
Kyoto Institute of Technology	Meiji University
Nagaoka University of Technology	Nara Institute of Science and Technology
Okayama University	Rikkyo University
Ritsumeikan Asia Pacific University	Ritsumeikan University
Shibaura Institute of Technology	Soka University
Sophia University	Tokyo University of Foreign Studies
Tokyo University of the Arts	Toyo University
Toyohashi University of Technology	University of Aizu, The

EXERCISE 1: DETERMINING YOUR APPROACH

As promised in the introduction, here is your Chapter One exercise. I highly recommend following along with these exercises as you go along, to accompany any notes you might have taken. By the end of this book, your exercises should provide you with an application plan that will help you decide what to do next.

You can fill out your answers in a notebook or download the exercise worksheets that go with the book at:

http://www.transenzjapan.com/bonusmms1/

In this first exercise, we are going to establish your application approach.

Your Degree

1. What degree do you want to earn by the end of your scholarship? (Master's / PhD / Professional Master's / Professional Doctorate / Research Student only)

2. What is the first degree you need to earn to get there?

3. Do you have a reason that you need to earn your degree quickly and return to your home country (e.g. if you are on a leave of absence from work)?

4. Are you applying to repeat a degree that you have already earned? If so, why?

Your Application Schedule

5. What month is it as you are reading this?

Ideally, you should start preparing for your application up

to 6 months or more before the application deadline.
If it is between December to May*, you should consider
applying for the Embassy Recommendation first.
If it is between June to November*, you should consider
applying for the University Recommendation first.
(*If it is late May or late November, you may not have enough
time, check your individual embassy or university for more
information)

6. Based on the explanation above, what application
process are you going to apply for first? (Embassy / University)

Your Goals and Resources

7. What is your life goal that will be helped by earning the
degree you wrote above via the MEXT Scholarship? (It can be a
broad goal for now, we will refine it later!)

8. What practical resources do you have that you can use to
aid your scholarship application?

☐Contact with your academic adviser from your last degree
☐Contact with a professor in your field in Japan
☐A strong relationship with an academic professional who can
review your Field of Study
☐Access to a university library
☐Contact with someone who has won the scholarship in the
past
☐Contact with a friend or professional who can proofread your
application
☐Other

CHAPTER TWO:
Successful Applicant Mindset

Shouldn't it be enough just to be an outstanding student with an excellent research plan?

Maybe it should, but the fact is that it is not enough. You might have the best research plan in the world. But if you cannot communicate it to the scholarship reviewers, or if you do not meet their expectations for communication and courtesy, then your chances of winning the scholarship will sink faster than a raft in a typhoon.

If you were just trying to get in to a Japanese graduate school you could do that on the strength of your academic record, alone. But you are applying for the MEXT scholarship. You are competing with the best scholars from around the world to earn one of a few scholarship slots. You need to stand out, and that means taking not only your research, but the application process, itself, seriously.

You *can* do this. You can set yourself out from the crowd. All it takes is deliberate focus and a little extra work.

The first thing we are going to cover together is how you can take a professional approach to the scholarship application. Do not just skip over this chapter because it does not talk about the practical application forms or where and when to submit your application. We will cover that later, but your attitude toward the application process comes first.

Your mindset is the most important thing to get in order before you start your application. If you are ready to approach this application professionally and you understand what you need to do to succeed, then you will set yourself up for success that will improve the effectiveness of everything else you do. On the other hand, if you are not prepared to take the application seriously, then no amount of advice I can give will make much of a difference for your chances.

BE CONFIDENT

Have any of these questions crossed your mind?

- I don't have any publications.. Will I still have a chance?
- I've never been to Japan. Will that put me at a disadvantage?
- I don't have any professional experience, or TA experience, etc. Is that going to hurt my application?
- I'm majoring in humanities. Can I even compete with engineering or science majors?

Hundreds of applicants have emailed me with those questions or posted them in the comments on my website over the years. If that's you then here is your answer:

You absolutely still have as much of a chance as anyone, because what you did in the past is not nearly as important as what you will do in the future.

The vast majority of applicants I worked with - including the majority of successful applicants - were applying while they were still students, with no publications, no professional experience, and no previous trips to Japan.

Your past experience is valuable if you can leverage it to show the reviewers how it will help you be a better scholar. But even if you do not have the specific experiences I listed above, you surely have some experience you can leverage. We will cover specific strategies later in chapter 4. For now, the important takeaway is not to let your past experience or lack of experience hold you back.

While competition for the MEXT scholarship is high, ultimately, what will determine your success is how hard you are willing to work to make your application as strong as possible.

Less than 5% of international students in Japan are MEXT scholars. It may seem like you have to get lucky to become one of those few. But as film producer Samuel Goldwyn said, "The harder I work, the luckier I get."

Decide that you are going to put in the work to earn this scholarship and you can be confident that you have every chance of success.

BE PROFESSIONAL

If someone offered you a job that would pay 10,000,000 yen (approximately $100,000 USD), plus give you the chance to earn a Master's Degree and Doctoral Degree for free, how would you talk to that person? How much care would you give to the job application form? How would you act in the interview?

We covered the benefits in the previous chapter, so you know the MEXT scholarship can be worth that much, just counting your monthly stipend. Plus, the degrees will continue to pay off for you for the rest of your life with job opportunities in the future.

So, how would you approach this offer?

Surprisingly, a lot of applicants do not take it seriously at all. They are careless or even rude to the reviewers and staff. They are disorganized and come off as lazy and whiny.

You want to approach every interaction and every document you submit as if that one thing could make the difference between receiving 10,000,000 yen or not. If you adopt a professional manner, you will be ahead of a significant number of applicants. And the more you take the application and yourself seriously and professionally, the more likely the embassy and university staff are to treat you the same way.

Here are a few key areas you need to be sure to get right:

1. Professional Communication and Appearance

I used to get emails like the message below:

"Dear Sensei,

I am an eager and active young student from country X and I want to study at your university with the MEXT scholarship.

I would be honored if you could nominate me for the scholarship.

Looking forward to your urgent reply.

————

Set from my iPhone"

It almost takes work to be so rude and unprofessional in such a short email. I will include a whole chapter on professional email courtesy in Book 3 of this series, but here are some of the problems with this message:

- **Dear Sensei:** The applicant did not even bother to look up the name and title of the person he was sending to. Furthermore, he sent it to an admin office, so the person reading it was not a "sensei", anyway.
- **Multiple Addresses:** You cannot tell this from the excerpt above, but I would get emails like this with 10 or more universities in the "To" line of the email.
- **No Knowledge of the University:** Nothing in this email indicates that the applicant has taken the time to research the degrees offered at the university, the research, or the professors. He is clearly just seeking a scholarship and has nothing to offer in return.
- **Urgent Reply:** On top of everything else, the applicant is being demanding of the reader's time after clearly taking no time to do any work himself.
- **No Name:** Even if your email address is your name, it is rude to not write your name in the signature of your

message. This is not an SMS.
- **Sent from my iPhone:** The applicant could not be bothered to sit down at a computer and type a proper email. He probably sent this message while he was bored waiting for a bus.

Email etiquette may be different from country to country, but as a professional, it is your responsibility to find out what the expectations are from the perspective of the person on the receiving end and to live up to them. Do not worry, I have you covered!

Presenting a professional appearance in physical interviews - and even when submitting your application documents at the embassy - is equally important. Go in there like you are walking into a corporate job interview worth 10 million yen. (Yes, I keep repeating that number. It is important to remember what is at stake!)

2. Professional Preparation

Would you walk into a 10,000,000 yen job interview without having researched the company and its expectations in advance? I hope not. You would know everything there is to know about the company's mission and history. You would know what they are looking for in an employee, and you would know what questions and expectations to anticipate and how you plan to respond.

You would also know which of your strengths you need to emphasize to give you the best chance at getting the job.

You should approach the scholarship in the exact same way. Taking the application seriously means knowing the goals and desired outcomes of the scholarship program from MEXT's perspective. It means knowing what the universities and your potential adviser wants out of its students. And it means being prepared to address those questions in every document and interview.

We will cover this more in the chapter on your application strategy later in this book. In later books, we will come back to this as you write your Field of Study and Research Program Plan and prepare for your interviews, too.

3. Timeliness

Timeliness is the cornerstone of professionalism. You probably already know that turning in an assignment late at university can result in reduced points or zero credit. In the professional world, timeliness is more important. If you fail to deliver goods and services on time, you can lost contracts or lose your job.

In Japan, timeliness is all but sacred.

In 2017, an incident made international news when a Japanese train departed the station 20 seconds early. The company apologized profusely for the error, which was abnormal and unacceptable in Japan. However, what made the story international news was the comparison between the Japanese system and the rest of the world. People were shocked that 20 seconds was such a big deal. It is.

When we accepted scholarship applications in person at my university in Japan, the submission deadline was 17:00:00 according to our atomic clock. We had staff standing by at the door as the time approached and as soon as the clocked ticked over to the hour, we would lock it, even if a student was running toward the door and three steps away. No excuses were ever accepted.

As you go through this application process, do not procrastinate. If the embassy or university contacts you, you should be prepared to reply within 24 hours at all times. And not from your iPhone, like the message above. Even if you cannot answer their question or submit the document they requested within 24 hours, it is polite to reply to acknowledge the message and, tell them you are working on it, and let them know when you will submit it.

On the other hand, do not hold the university or embassy to the same expectations. The embassy and university are the ones who get to decide who earns the scholarship. They do not have to be as polite or courteous to you as you have to be to them. Sure, in an ideal world, they would be. But understand, too, that you are one of probably hundreds of applicants they are dealing with at once, and they simply cannot get back to everyone as quickly as they want to.

Even though it might grate on you to have to wait, part of being professional means understanding their situation and respecting their time. And of course, knowing when it is time to send a polite reminder, as well.

A professional mindset is a minimum requirement to succeed in the MEXT scholarship application. Approach this scholarship with the same professional mindset that you would take for a 10,000,000 yen job application and you will already be at an advantage over a significant number of applicants!

DON'T BE COCKY

The single greatest failure I have seen among applicants - the reason most eliminated themselves from competition   is thinking only about themselves.

The last step we are going to cover in your mindset is to grasp the bigger picture. You need to think about the other students applying and what they are doing. You need to think about each person that you talk to during the application process and what their perspective is. Understanding your place in the greater system is going to help you get much closer to success.

Thinking About Other Applicants

The competition level for the MEXT scholarship is high. Expect to have anywhere between 10 to 20 or more applicants for every scholarship slot available.

I do not want you to let this get you down. I want you to use it as motivation. Use it as motivation whenever you are thinking about cutting corners, or considering a document "good enough." Think about how much extra effort you need to put in to beat out the other applicants, and make sure you are not eliminating yourself from competition by giving up too easily.

Thinking About the Reviewers

Almost everyone you interact with during the application process is looking for reasons to eliminate applicants. Make sure you leave them with the impression that you are one that they want to keep around.

Because of the competition numbers I mentioned above, the reviewers at the embassy and even at the university cannot hope to give every application the attention that it deserves. They have to narrow down the applicants to those who have the most promise as quickly and efficiently as possible. Really, even then, they will not be able to give every applicant and application the attention you think you deserve.

Throughout the application process, but especially at the early stages, understand that you are probably not going to be able to get the personal attention you want. To the reviewers at this stage, you are just one of a sea of applicants and they may well be operating by the standard Japanese rule of fairness:

If they cannot offer something to all applicants at once, they will not offer it to any at all.

Here are some examples of how applicants typically go wrong in their relationship building with th reviewers, and what you can do to avoid the mistakes.

How to Kill Your Application Chances

- **Applying when not eligible.**
  Obviously, this is the first elimination criteria. In the next chapter in this book, we will walk through your eligibility criteria together so you can be sure this will not be a problem for you.

- **Unprofessional communication.**
  We covered this briefly above and will go into detail in Book 3 of this series, when we discuss reaching out to your prospective adviser In my experience, this is a particular problem in email communications with your university. Email can lead to miscommunication between two people who share a common first language and cultural background and you will not even have that commonality to help you. Re-read your email before you send it to make sure there are no areas where you are inviting misunderstanding.

- **Asking questions you should be able to find the answers to yourself.**
  Honestly, I see this all the time on my own website, and it drives me crazy. You do not need my approval to get the scholarship, but my concern is that if these applicants treat the actual application process like they treat the resources I've created, they are going to crash and burn.

  Do not jump straight to sending a question by email until you have reviewed the embassy or university's website and made sure that the answer is not written there. Otherwise, you risk showing them that you are too lazy or incompetent to do basic research on your own. And when you *do* write an email (because there will be some things that are unclear in their instructions, I can practically guarantee it), be sure to indicate that you have researched the question as best as possible on your own, but were unable to find the answer. You are applying to be a research student. The embassy and university staff will expect you to act like one. By taking the initiative to invest in yourself with a book on the application process, you are prepared to do what it takes to improve your application, but make sure that you carry that mindset forward in your interaction with the university.

- **Asking for exceptions.**
  Applicants used to email me all the time to ask for exceptions to the application requirements or to the application process. My answer was no. It had to be, unless there was a specific alternative pre-approved. For one thing, the requirements are set by MEXT and nobody at the university had the authority to override them. And for another, I had about 200 applicants who *were* willing and able to meet the requirements. I had no reason to spend any time on someone who could not or did not want to.

  Do not ask for exceptions or exemptions, if you can possibly avoid it. And if you do, make sure you provide a compelling reason why the situation is beyond your control (for example, if your recommender insists on sending the letter directly to the embassy/university) or why you should be considered and why it is worth the university or embassy's time and effort to consider you for special treatment. If you must ask for an exception, you should provide the embassy or university with an alternative that is easy and convenient for them to accept.

- **Tardiness.**
  We covered this in the section on being professional, so I will not spend too much time on it. One of the easiest way to get yourself eliminated is to miss a deadline. Keep in mind

that most Japanese deadlines are "arrive by" deadlines, not postmark deadlines. If something is due by mail, then it must be in the university's hands by 17:00 on the deadline day, not just in the mail. Also, keep the time difference in mind! If you are communicating with the university, their time zone is ahead of yours and they will consider the cut off time and date according to their clock, not yours. Submit early to avoid any possible deadline misses.

In general, remember the numbers. Think about the competition and the sheer volume of applicants that the university and embassy have to deal with. If you are ever in doubt, ask yourself if your action is going to put you ahead of or behind your competition. If you think about the bigger picture in this way, act professional, and maintain the confidence that you can win this scholarship, you should be set up for success!

Now that we have you mindset in order, let's go cover that first item on the list: making sure you are eligible to apply.

EXERCISE 2: MINDSET

Let's stop now and make sure you have your mindset right. We are not going to go into too much detail, because we will save that for the chapter on your application strategy later. For now, I just want to know that you are with me. I believe you can do this. I want to make sure you believe it, too, and that you are willing to do what it takes to make this work.

As before, you can fill out your answers in a notebook or download the exercise worksheets that go with the book at:

http://www.transenzjapan.com/bonusmms1/

Confidence

This is an exercise I still use every time I think I don't have what it takes. It always helps me at least to pretend that I have the confidence I need long enough to get the job done.

1. Are you concerned that you won't be able to compete for the MEXT scholarship?

2. Why? What disadvantages do you think you have? Be specific.

3. Do you think no other applicant has those same problems or concerns?

4. If every other applicant is human, too, with strengths and weaknesses, what strengths do you have that can set you apart from them? (Here's one: You're the kind of person who is willing to invest the time and money in yourself to succeed, as evidenced by the fact that you're reading this book and following through with the exercises!)

5. If you apply for the scholarship and don't get it, what's the worst that could happen to you? Again, be specific.

6. Is that worse than what happens if you never apply?

Professionalism

7. Imagine *you* were offering an award worth 10,000,000 yen. How would you expect applicants to write their emails?

8. What characteristics would you look for in their plans?

9. How would you expect applicants to dress and prepare mentally for an interview?

10. On a more practical matter, how often do you check your email and what alerts and systems can you set up to make sure you notice important messages?

Humility

11. Do you need any special consideration during the application process? (e.g. no language proficiency scores, financial assistance for sending materials or traveling)

12. What can you do on your own to overcome those challenges?

13. Do you communicate well in writing in English?

14. Is there someone you could ask to test your emails to the embassy and university to make sure your message gets across? Preferably, choose someone who is timely, reliable, and not afraid to give you their frank opinion.

15. Are you the kind of person who immediately asks questions or do you do research on your own? If you are tempted to ask questions before doing your own searching, what can you do to help yourself overcome that problem?

CHAPTER THREE:
Eligibility

It goes without saying that you must be eligible to apply.

While there are some exceptions built into the rules, there is zero possibility of obtaining a personal exception to the eligibility criteria otherwise. So, if you do not meet the requirements we will discuss in this chapter, then you will not be able to apply.

If that's the case for you, I'm sorry, but at least by finding out at this stage, you can save yourself considerable time and money on the application process and focus your efforts on another goal.

The MEXT scholarship eligibility criteria can be confusing. Some criteria, such as the minimum GPA, are only explained in Japanese. Some criteria do not seem have any objective measurement. In this chapter, I will explain each criteria in detail to make them clear. I will start with the eligibility criteria as written in the application guidelines, then explain what it means to you.

The eligibility criteria below are based on the most recent requirements as of the time of publishing: the 2019 Embassy Recommendation eligibility requirements and 2018 University Recommendation eligibility requirements.

A Note About Language and Translation

For the Embassy Recommendation application process, MEXT publishes the application guidelines, including the eligibility requirements, in English, so I will use their wording directly. For the University Recommendation application process, MEXT only publishes the guidelines in Japanese. In cases where the university guidelines are different from the embassy and no official translation exists, I will provide my own translation and let you know when I do so.

Order of Eligibility Criteria

Instead of following the order in MEXT's guidelines, I will

group the eligibility criteria by similar types and address them in order from easiest to most difficult to assess. If you are trying to follow along with the actual application guidelines, this may jump around a little bit, but I will cover everything.

ACADEMIC BACKGROUND AND DEGREE COMPLETION

The Requirement

This is one section where the Embassy and University processes differ.

MEXT Explanation for Embassy Recommended scholarship application process (from the 2019 application cycle):

Eligible applicants satisfy the qualification requirements for admission to a Master's degree course or a Doctoral degree course at a Japanese graduate school. (Includes applicants who are certainly expected to satisfy the requirements by the time of enrollment.)

Students must satisfy any one of the following eligibility criteria.

1. *Master's program / Doctoral program (first phase)*
    1. *Japanese university graduates.*
    2. *Students that have been conferred their Bachelor's degree through the National Institution for Academic Degrees and Quality Enhancement of Higher Education (NIAD-QE).*
    3. *Students who have completed 16 years of school education in countries other than Japan.*
    4. *Students who have completed a program with the standard study period of three years or more at universities or equivalent educational institutions in*

countries other than Japan and received a degree equivalent to a Bachelor's degree.

5. *Students who have completed 16 years of education at education institutions in Japan recognized as having overseas undergraduate programs.*
6. *Students who have completed designated professional training college courses.*
7. *Students recognized as having academic abilities equivalent to or better than university graduates in an individual entrance qualification examination conducted by a graduate school, and who have reached 22 years of age.*

2. *Doctoral program (second phase)*
   1. *Students with a Japanese Master's degree or students with a Japanese professional degree.*
   2. *Students who have been awarded with an overseas degree equivalent to a Master's degree or professional degree.*
   3. *Students who have completed graduate programs at education institutions in Japan recognized as having overseas graduate programs and who have obtained a degree equivalent to a Master's degree or professional degree.*
   4. *Students who have graduated from universities and have been involved in research study at universities or research centers (including overseas universities and research centers) for two years or more, and recognized as having academic competency equivalent to persons with a Master's degree by the graduate school.*
   5. *Students recognized as having academic abilities equivalent to or better than Master's degree or professional degree holders in an individual entrance qualification examination conducted by the graduate school, and who have reached 24 years of age.*

3. *Doctoral program (faculties of medicine, dentistry,*

veterinary sciences and certain pharmaceutical programs)
If you apply to a program in medicine, dentistry,
veterinary medicine or certain pharmaceutical sciences,
you are required to confirm directly with the school of your
choice before applying.

MEXT Explanation for University Recommendation scholarship application process (from the 2018 application cycle):

Applicants must meet the entrance requirements for a Master's degree or Doctoral degree program at a Japanese university (including those who do not meet the requirements at the time of application but will do so before arriving in Japan).*
*My translation

Yes, the requirements for the University Recommendation are *much* simpler. That's because you are being nominated to MEXT by the university directly, so MEXT assumes that the university has already determined that you are qualified for the degree program.

Interpreting the Requirements

The basic rule of thumb for your academic background is that you must meet all of the requirements necessary to enroll in the same level degree program in a university in your home country.

If you are applying for the University Recommendation, the process is straightforward. If the university determines that your academic background is sufficient, that is all you need. In most cases, that means that if you are applying for a Master's degree, you need to have finished your Bachelor's degree (or be expected to finish it before arriving in Japan). If you are applying for a Doctoral degree, then you would have to have finished or be expected to finish your Master's degree, first.

If you are applying for the Embassy Recommendation, then the the most relevant requirements are number 4 for Master's degree applicants and number 2 for Doctoral degree applicants. Those requirements state that you are eligible if you have completed - or are expected to complete - a degree equivalent to a Bachelor's degree (for Master's applicants) or Master's degree (for Doctoral applicants) overseas.

When MEXT says "expected to complete", it means that you are still enrolled now, but will complete all requirements for your current degree before you come to Japan.

If you are applying for medical, dental, pharmaceutical, or veterinary programs, you would need to have approval from the university you intend to apply to in advance, regardless of whether you plan to apply for Embassy or University Recommendation.

Doctoral Program Phases

In the eligibility criteria above, you will see a reference to the first phase and second phase of a Doctoral program. In Japanese, there are different words for a terminal Master's degree (studies that end at a Master's degree with no Doctoral degree offered at that institution) and studies that offer the possibility of continuing on to a Doctoral degree. In most cases in English, both are translated to "Master's Degree".

Whenever you see "Doctoral Degree (first phase)" you can assume that it means "Master's Degree".

BASIC ELIGIBILITY CRITERIA: MEASURABLE

There are a few basic, measurable eligibility requirements that are quick and easy to check off, so let's cover those, first.

Nationality

The Requirement

The requirements for the Embassy Recommendation and University Recommendation are almost identical:

Applicants must have the nationality of a country that has diplomatic relations with Japan. An applicant who has Japanese nationality at the time of application is not eligible. However, persons with dual nationality who hold Japanese nationality and whose place of residence at the time of application is outside of Japan are eligible to apply as long as they choose the nationality of the foreign country and renounce their Japanese nationality by the date of their arrival in Japan. The First Screening must be conducted at the Japanese diplomatic mission in the country of which the applicant chooses the nationality.

The only difference between the two versions is the last sentence above. Obviously, for the University Recommendation, applicant screening is conducted at the university, not the Japanese diplomatic mission.

Interpreting the Requirement

Japan recognizes and has diplomatic relations with almost all recognized, independent states. It does not have formal diplomatic relations with Taiwan, North Korea, or disputed states such as South Ossetia, etc., so applicants with those nationalities are not able to apply. (For Taiwan, however, there is an independent organization that offers a nearly identical scholarship).

To determine whether Japan has diplomatic relations with your country, the best approach is to search the Ministry of Foreign Affairs' list of Japanese diplomatic missions abroad:

http://www.transenzjapan.com/embassies/

I recommend using the search (Control-F) function on that page, since Japan might not list your country under the region/continent that you are used to. For example, you will find Tajikistan in the column for Europe.

In some cases, Japan may have formal diplomatic relations with your country, but may not have a physical embassy or consulate located in your country (or may have moved out of your country due to war, etc.). In that case, there will still be a link on the page above for your country and that will tell you where the Japanese embassy to your country is located. For example, the "Japanese Embassy in Yemen" was relocated to Riyadh, Saudi Arabia in 2015. Applicants from Yemen are still eligible, but would apply via the embassy in Riyadh for the scholarship.

Japanese Dual Nationality

If you have dual nationality including Japanese nationality, you are not eligible to apply unless you surrender your Japanese nationality. Of course, once you pass the age of 20, Japan "requires" you to choose to surrender either your Japanese or foreign nationality, so in theory you would have already had to make that choice. In practice, however, there is no enforcement method other than things like this scholarship application process.

Surrendering your nationality is a much larger decision and process than just applying for a scholarship. If you are in that situation, I would recommend that you think about the future costs and benefits, as well, and proceed carefully.

Age

The Requirement

The requirements for the Embassy Recommendation and University Recommendation are almost identical:

MEXT explanation for Embassy Recommendation scholarship application process (from the 2019 application cycle):

Applicants, in principle, must have been born on or after April 2, 1984*. Exceptions are limited to cases in which MEXT deems that the applicant could not apply within the eligible age limit due to the situation or circumstances of the applicant's country (military service obligation, loss of educational opportunities due to disturbances of war, etc.) Personal circumstances (financial situation, family circumstances, state of health, circumstances related to applicant's university or place of employment, etc.) will not be considered for exceptions.

MEXT explanation for University Recommendation scholarship application process (from the 2018 application cycle):

Applicants, in principle, must have been born on or before April 2, 1983.* Exceptions will be granted in cases where MEXT has determined that applicants were not able to apply during the years they would have been eligible due to conditions in their home country (such as mandatory military service or the suspension of higher education due to war, revolt, etc.) Exceptions will not be made for personal circumstances (such as economic situation, family-related matters, health, or limitations imposed by home country universities or employers) under any circumstances. Exceptions to the age requirement will also be granted to applicants who have completed the MEXT Young Leaders Program and wish to move on to a Doctoral degree, provided that that they apply within five years of completing the Young Leaders Program.**
**My translation.

*The specific year changes each year and is always 35 years before the year that the scholarship starts. Since the descriptions above come from different years, the exact year is different.

The only difference between the two criteria above is the exception for graduates of the Young Leaders Program, which only exists for the University Recommendation.

Interpreting the Requirements

The chances are well above 99% that the exceptions do not apply to you. So, all we need to do is calculate your age.

As I mentioned above, you must be born no later than April 2 of the year 35 years before the year you will start your studies in Japan. The numbers above are from the application process for scholars who will arrive in 2018 and 2019. To find the correct year for your application, subtract 35 from the year you will *arrive in Japan.* The year that you will arrive in Japan is typically one year later than the year you are applying.

For example, if you are applying in 2018 and will start your studies in 2019, you would have to be born no later than April 2, 1984. (2019 - 35 = 1984)

Health

The Requirement

The requirements for the Embassy Recommendation and University Recommendation are almost identical:

MEXT explanation for Embassy Recommendation scholarship application process (from the 2019 application cycle):

Applicants must submit a health certificate in the prescribed format signed by a physician attesting that the applicant has no physical or mental conditions hindering the applicant's study in Japan.

MEXT explanation for University Recommendation scholarship application process (from the 2018 application cycle):

Applicants must be determined by the nominating university to have no physical or mental conditions hindering the applicant's study in Japan.*
*My translation.

The primary difference here is that there is a required medical form format for the Embassy Recommendation scholarship. MEXT does not require a specific form for the University Recommendation, leaving it up to each individual university to decide. Many universities will use the Embassy format, anyway.

Interpreting the Requirements

Essentially, you must have a physician's certification that you do not require any ongoing care or medication that would require you to remain in your home country under treatment.

I have never seen or heard of a student getting eliminated for this requirement. (However, I did once have a student who forged the Medical Form because he did not want to pay a doctor for the exam, so that student was eliminated).

The only situations this might apply to are ongoing recovery from a serious disease or injury that requires regular care and therapy and/or would prevent you from flying. Obviously, being hospitalized long-term would also eliminate you. However, since the application process can take more than a year, the chances are good that you would have time to complete your care in the meantime, if it was not a chronic condition.

If you have an ongoing condition that you can manage on your own without regular care from the same physician, that should not be a problem. Even in cases where you need regular check-ups, but any doctor in the field could do it (for example, regular blood tests), that would not be an obstacle to studying in Japan. It may be a challenge to you personally, as finding medical personnel that can give care in English can be challenging in some parts of the country, but it would not affect your eligibility. I will discuss medical care in Japan in Book 7 of this series.

Prescription medication would also not impact your eligibility, but you would be responsible for securing it from your home country prior to departure. I will cover more on medication in Book 6 of this series, when we talk about preparing to move to Japan.

BASIC ELIGIBILITY CRITERIA: UNMEASURABLE

In addition to the measurable criteria, there are some "eligibility criteria" that cannot be objectively measured.

While there is no specific standard to meet here, you should be aware of these criteria as you may get asked about them during the application or interview process. Depending on your answer, they could get you eliminated, if the reviewer gets the wrong impression from you.

Language Ability

The Requirement
This is another section where the Embassy and University processes differ, at least as of 2018/2019.

MEXT Explanation for Embassy Recommendation scholarship application process (from the 2019 application cycle):

Applicants must be willing to learn Japanese. Applicants must be interested in Japan and be willing to deepen their understanding of Japan after arriving in Japan. Applicants must also have the ability to do research and adapt to living in Japan.

MEXT Explanation for University Recommendation scholarship application process (from the 2018 application cycle):

Applicants must have the requisite knowledge of either English or Japanese to be able to undertake education and complete research at a university level. While it will not be considered in the screening for this year, to the maximum degree possible applicants should undertake an external language proficiency test (for English: TOEFL, IELTS, etc.; For Japanese: JLPT, etc.) to demonstrate their language ability. However, for fields of study for which Japanese language fluency is required (Japanese language, Japanese literature, Japanese history, Japanese law, etc.), applicants with insufficient proficiency in Japanese will not be selected*
*My translation.

There is clearly a major difference here in the language proficiency requirements. This is in part due to the nature of the application process. If you apply for the Embassy Recommendation, you will take a language proficiency test there after you pass the document screening, so they do not require you to have a formal test such as TOEFL or the JLPT.

Interpreting the Requirements: Embassy

The eligibility requirement for the embassy cannot be measured. There is no objective way to tell if you are "willing to learn Japanese" or "interested in Japan". Given that you are applying for a graduate program in Japan, that's more or less assumed!

The only way you can run afoul of this requirement on the Embassy Recommendation path is if you explicitly say in your field of study and research program plan or during your interview that you are not interested in Japan or that you refuse to learn Japanese. That should be easy to avoid.

Language ability also comes into play in the the "Field of Study" eligibility criteria that we will discuss a little later.

It is important to note that if you are applying by Embassy Recommendation, you are also going to have to meet the universities' requirements when you apply for a Letter of Acceptance later in the process. While this is not a matter of "eligibility", just be aware that you may need language proficiency test scores, after all, if your university demands them. It's always better to have them than not.

Interpreting the Requirements: University

2018 was the first year that MEXT added the requirement that applicants should have official language proficiency test scores. Since this was the first year and there was no advance notice, MEXT did not make it an absolute requirement but said that applicants should have test scores to the maximum degree possible. It is reasonable to assume that in future years, MEXT will *require* that universities collect official language proficiency test scores from applicants.

I have mentioned this before, but please be sure to download your bonus materials and sign up for my mailing list so that I can let you know as requirements change in the future!

http://www.transenzjapan.com/bonusmms1/

Even if they do make test score submission mandatory, it is very likely that MEXT will not require a particular score on the proficiency test. They will only require that you have taken one and that the university confirms your test score is high enough to complete your studies. Practically speaking, language proficiency requirements vary from field to field regardless of whether you are talking about Japanese or English. In general, social sciences and humanities fields will want to see higher language proficiency than STEM.

Make sure that your test scores are official! Your university or language schools in your city may offer prediction tests, equivalency tests, or institutional tests for much lower cost, but there's a good chance that these would not be accepted. MEXT will want to see official TOEFL iBT or IELTS scores. Yes, these are more expensive, but the MEXT scholarship is a merit-based scholarship, not a need-based scholarship. Arguments that you cannot afford the test are not going to get you any traction.

Exceptions for Native Speakers?

In the past, I have seen some exceptions for native English speakers from countries that speak only English. That means the US, UK, Canada, Australia, and New Zealand.

For countries like India, Bangladesh, Ghana, etc., where English is the official language of education, applicants were not granted exceptions. I'm sorry to say it, but almost every university in Japan now has seen at least one student who graduated from a degree program supposedly taught entirely in English in one of these countries who had no English language ability, whatsoever. Because of those experiences, universities have no option but to assume that it is possible to graduate from these English-speaking programs by getting extra assistance from professors in their native language.

If you are not originally from one of the five English-speaking countries I listed above, but you are enrolled in a university there or graduated from there within the last two years, then you may be able to submit a copy of the English language proficiency scores that you sent to your last university when you enrolled, rather than having to take a new test.

There are also cases where native speakers might not be exempt from taking language proficiency tests!

I have heard of applicants in the UK, who were born and raised there, having to take the Embassy's English language proficiency test during the screening. I also knew a university that had literally never had a native English speaker apply to one of its programs before and so had not written in an exception for native speakers. Since that university could not change its application guidelines on the fly, it ended up forcing an American applicant to take the TOEFL.

Finding Testing Centers and Dates

The links below should help you identify the next available tests in your area.

- TOEFL iBT Test Dates and Locations:
  http://www.transenzjapan.com/toefl/
- IELTS Test Dates and Locations:
  http://www.transenzjapan.com/ielts/
- JLPT Test Dates and Locations:
  http://www.transenzjapan.com/jlpt/

Willingness to Get Involved

The Requirement

The requirements for the Embassy Recommendation and University Recommendation are identical:

MEXT Scholarship will be granted those who are willing to contribute to mutual understanding between Japan and their home country by participating in activities at schools and communities during their study in Japan while contributing to the internationalization of Japan. They shall also make efforts to promote relations between the home country and Japan by maintaining close relations with the university attended after graduation, cooperating with the conducting of surveys and questionnaires, and cooperating with relevant projects and events conducted by Japanese diplomatic missions after they return to their home countries.

Interpreting the Requirement

This is not necessarily something that can be objectively measured - at least, not until well after you are awarded the scholarship. However, it is something you should keep in mind and address directly in your application.

When writing the research timeline portion of the Field of Study and Research Program Plan, include references to finding local community activities to get involved in and participating in interaction. If there is some way to leverage your research to benefit the local community, such as giving presentations or lessons to community groups, that is a great thing to identify. But even if your research does not directly relate to community interaction, it is still beneficial to make it clear that you plan to actively seek opportunities to contribute to the community while in Japan.

In the Embassy Recommendation application process, you will also likely have a chance in the interview to talk about how you will adjust to Japan and this is another good opportunity to mention your plans to proactively get involved and contribute to the community and mutual understanding.

You do not need to spend much time dwelling on this subject, a casual reference is all you will need.

DISQUALIFICATION CRITERIA

There are several disqualification criteria that will eliminate you from the application process and can result in cancellation of your scholarship if they are discovered after you arrive in Japan.

If your scholarship is canceled after arriving in Japan because you are found to meet one of the disqualification criteria, it would be canceled under the condition of you "voluntarily withdrawing" from the scholarship. In that case, you would not need to pay back any scholarship amount awarded.

All of these criteria are straightforward and easy to identify, so you do not need to worry about tricky definitions or gray areas. We will go through them once now so you can ensure you meet all the requirements and have nothing to worry about.

For all other eligibility requirements we cover, you have to meet the criteria described to be eligible. However, for the disqualification criteria, the MEXT guidelines write them in a way that anyone who meets the description is *ineligible.*

Military Affiliation

The Requirement

The requirements for the Embassy Recommendation and University Recommendation are identical:

Those who are military personnel or military civilian employees at the time of their arrival in Japan.

Interpreting the Requirement

As long as you are not employed by the military as an active-duty soldier or a civilian employee, you are eligible.

If you previously served in the military but have been discharged (even if you are in obligatory reserve status) or if you previously worked for the military as a civilian but are no longer under contract with them, you are eligible.

Arrival in Japan

The Requirement

The requirements for the Embassy Recommendation and University Recommendation are identical:

Those who cannot arrive in Japan during the period designated by MEXT or the accepting university.

Interpreting the Requirement

You cannot delay your arrival or defer your scholarship award for any reason.

There are two things you need to consider here:

1. There must not be anything in your home country that would prevent you from leaving on schedule, and
2. There must be no reason why you would be ineligible to enter Japan.

If you are currently employed, you will have to be able to leave your job and arrive in Japan per the dates specified by MEXT and the university. You cannot make changes to your arrival dates due to work circumstances.

The same goes if you are still enrolled in school. If there is some last event you want to attend at your previous university, such as a degree conferment ceremony, you would not be able to delay your trip to Japan for that.

One other precaution to look out for here is that there are some countries that do not allow their citizens (or in some cases government employees) free access to their own passports. If you need permission from your home country government to obtain your passport and leave the country, you will have to secure that in advance.

Regarding entering Japan, if you have been deported from

Japan in the past or departed under a Departure Order, there is a specific period during which you are not allowed to re-enter the country. You are not eligible to apply for the MEXT scholarship if it would mean entering Japan again during that period. But, hopefully, that does not apply to anyone reading this!

Past Scholarship Receipt

The Requirement

The requirements for the Embassy Recommendation and University Recommendation are almost identical:

Those who are previous grantees of Japanese Government (MEXT) Scholarship programs (including those who withdraw from the scholarship program after the arrival in Japan), but does not have educational research experience exceeding more than three years from the month following the final payment of the previous scholarship to the month when the payment of this scholarship begins. This does not apply to the past grantees of Japanese Studies scholarship nor Japan-Korea Joint Government Scholarship Program for the Students in Science and Engineering Departments who have graduated or are going to graduate from universities in their home countries and past participants in the Young Leaders Program. The MEXT Honors Scholarship is not one of the MEXT Scholarship Programs.

The description above was taken from the 2019 Embassy Recommendation guidelines, which are the most recent, and there are two minor differences from the most recent University Recommendation Guidelines, but both appear to be clarifications:

- (including those who withdraw from the scholarship program after the arrival in Japan)

- The MEXT Honors Scholarship is not one of the MEXT Scholarship Programs

These changes do not affect the meaning of the requirement.

Interpreting the Requirement

Past receipt of Japanese government scholarships *does not* include the JASSO scholarship or the MEXT Honors Scholarship, so if you received any of those scholarships in the past, you are still eligible.

You only need to be concerned if you received a MEXT scholarship in the past for degree-seeking studies in Japan.

This year, MEXT clarified the requirement to show that it applied even if you were awarded the scholarship but later withdrew *after* arrival in Japan. If for some reason you withdrew before arriving in Japan, then you would still be eligible. Remember that violating any of the eligibility criteria counts as "voluntary withdrawal" from the program.

The MEXT Japanese Studies Scholarship or the Japan Korea Joint Government Scholarship Program For The Students In Science and Engineering Departments are both scholarships that apply to students enrolled in overseas universities who study abroad in Japan for part of their degrees. As long as you have returned to your home country and university and graduated from that university (or, if you are still enrolled, will graduate from that university before coming to Japan), that will not impact your eligibility.

If you have received a MEXT scholarship for a degree in Japan, other than the Young Leaders Program, then you will need to prove that you have sufficient experience from the end of that degree to the start of your new studies in Japan.

"Educational or research experience" in this context

essentially means enrollment at a university. In Japan "educational" experience refers to undergraduate studies and "research" experience refers to graduate studies.

Working at a university or research facility as a faculty member or full-time researcher could also count. However, other employment would not count, even if you have more than three years.

Calculating Time between Programs

When calculating the time, you start counting from the first day you were enrolled/working in education or research or the first day of the month after your last scholarship payment, whichever comes later.

For example, let's say you competed a Bachelor's degree as a MEXT scholar and your last scholarship payment was in March 2016.

If you enrolled in a Master's degree program in April 2016 and were enrolled for three full years (finishing your degree in March 2019), then you would be eligible to apply for a new MEXT scholarship starting in April 2019.

If you started your Master's degree in May 2016 and finished in March 2019, you would not meet the requirement of three full years (two years, eleven months). You would need to gain another month of research experience, perhaps by working for your adviser for a month after graduation. If you were able to get that extra month, you would be eligible to apply for a scholarship starting after that month was over. Since MEXT scholarships only start in April or September/October, the earliest you could possible arrive in Japan as a MEXT scholars again would be September 2019.

If your experience is working as a faculty member or researcher at a university or research institute, then you would need to show 36 full months of employment after April 1, 2016 (assuming the dates above) before you would be eligible to arrive in Japan again.

In either case, you can start your application before meeting the three-full-years requirement, but you would have to meet that requirement before arriving in Japan.

Concurrent MEXT Scholarship Application

The Requirement

This requirement exists only for the University Recommendation process:

*Applicants who are simultaneously submitting another application for the MEXT scholarship for 2018.**
*My translation, based on the 2018 requirement.

Interpreting the Requirement

This eligibility requirement means that you are not allowed to apply to multiple universities for the University Recommendation MEXT scholarship application during the same year.

You *are* allowed to apply for the University Recommendation process if you previously applied for the Embassy Recommendation application process and did not pass the Primary Screening. If you have already been eliminated from the Embassy Recommendation, then you would not be considered to be applying simultaneously, since that application would have ended for you.

If you applied for the Embassy Recommendation and did pass the Primary Screening, then you would not be eligible to apply for the University Recommendation. But since you are essentially guaranteed to receive the scholarship if you pass the embassy's Primary Screening, there would be no point to applying to the university, as well.

Concurrent Enrollment in Japan

The Requirement

The requirements for the Embassy Recommendation and University Recommendation are identical:

Those who are already enrolled in a Japanese university with a residence status of "Student," or who are going to be enrolled, or plan to enroll, in a Japanese university as a privately-financed international student from the time of application to the MEXT scholarship program in the their home country until the commencement of the period for payment of the MEXT scholarship. However, this stipulation does not apply to privately-financed international students who, even though they are enrolled, or are planning to enroll, in a Japanese university, verifiably complete their studies before the start of the scholarship payment period, return to their home country at the time of the scholarship application, and newly acquire the "Student" residence status and come to Japan.

Interpreting the Requirement

If you are not enrolled in a Japanese university, and do not intend to enroll in a Japanese university before the start of your MEXT-funded studies, this eligibility requirement does not apply to you.

If you are currently a self-financed student (including students financed by any other scholarship scheme besides a Japanese government scholarship) at a Japanese university and will graduate and return to your home country before the start of your MEXT scholarship, you are also eligible.

If you are outside Japan, but want to come to Japan in the meantime to enroll in a Japanese university for any reason, such as language studies, you would have to show that the program you plan to enroll in will be complete before your scholarship starts and that you will return to your home country between the end of that program and the start of the MEXT scholarship.

Basically, this eligibility requirement means that you cannot use this application process to start funding a degree in Japan partway through and you cannot quit the program you are enrolled in and switch to a MEXT scholarship-funded program if you are selected. (If you plan to quit and switch, you have to do that before you start the application).

I have seen cases where students applied and were accepted to Japanese universities as self-financed students, but then declined to enroll and applied for the MEXT scholarship, instead. That would not affect your eligibility.

Concurrent Scholarship Receipt

The Requirement

The requirements for the Embassy Recommendation and University Recommendation are identical:

Those who are planning to receive scholarship money from an organization other than MEXT (including a government organization of the applicant's country) on top of the scholarship money provided by MEXT after the start of the scholarship payment period.

Interpreting the Requirement

This requirement means that you cannot accept other scholarships that cover your studies or living expenses during your time in Japan. If you win the MEXT scholarship, you must cancel your application for any other scholarships you were seeking and withdraw from any other scholarship programs that had already selected you. For MEXT scholars with families, this includes any scholarship programs awarded *to you* to help cover your family's expenses while living in Japan. It would not include scholarships awarded directly to your family members.

This requirement *does not* include grants for specific research or conference attendance. MEXT scholars are still eligible to apply for grants to fund costs for their research projects or to defray the cost of travel to or participation in conferences during their studies in Japan.

Failure to Graduate from Previous Degree

The Requirement

The requirements for the Embassy Recommendation and University Recommendation are identical:

Applicants who are expected to graduate at the time of application and cannot satisfy the qualifications and the conditions related to academic background by the deadline given.

Interpreting the Requirement

If you have already graduated from your last degree program, this requirement does not apply to you.

This requirement only applies to applicants who have not yet graduated from their last degree when applying for the MEXT scholarship. If you fail to complete your degree before coming to Japan for any reason, you would lose your eligibility and forfeit your scholarship.

Anyone who submits a "Certificate of Expected Graduation" during the application process will be required to show a "Certificate of Graduation" before starting their MEXT-funded studies.

A Certificate of Graduation does not need to be a diploma.

A letter from your university stating that you have completed all of your requirements and will be awarded your degree at the next graduation ceremony is sufficient.

Japanese Dual Nationality

The Requirement

The requirements for the Embassy Recommendation and University Recommendation are identical:

Holders of dual nationality at the time of application who cannot verify that they will give up Japanese nationality by the time of the arrival in Japan.

Interpreting the Requirement

This requirement only applies if one of your nationalities is Japanese. If you have, for example, Indian and UK citizenship, this does not apply!

If you are a Japanese citizen with dual citizenship, you must be able to prove that you will surrender your Japanese citizenship before arriving in Japan.

Note that you do not have to surrender it before applying or before receiving the results. So, if you can, set the date to surrender your citizenship after the MEXT results are released, so that you have time to change your mind if you are not awarded the scholarship!

Remember that these disqualification criteria will also result in your scholarship being canceled if you are discovered to be in violation during your studies in Japan. So, if you do not surrender your Japanese nationality and it is discovered later, you would lose the scholarship.

Residence Status Other Than Student

The Requirement

In 2019, this was only listed as a disqualification criteria for the Embassy Recommendation application process, but it is a requirement for the University Recommendation, as well. It is covered under other paperwork for the University, to be completed after arrival in Japan:

Those who change their residence status to that of other than "Student" after their arrival in Japan.

Interpreting the Requirement

As a MEXT scholar, you will apply for and receive a "Student" visa before coming to Japan and will be on a "Student" residence status throughout the time of your studies.

There is really no reason you would change during your studies. Even if you marry a Japanese citizen, you would have to stay a "Student" until the end of your degree and change to a "Spouse" status after the last scholarship payment.

The only time this criteria becomes an issue is when students are in their last month or two of their scholarship and have found a job in Japan that they want to start immediately after graduation. In order to work in Japan after graduation, you would need to change to a working residence status. However, as a MEXT scholar, you must not do so until after you have signed for your last scholarship payment, even if your employer wants you to change earlier than that.

Research or Internship Outside Japan

The Requirement

The requirements for the Embassy Recommendation and University Recommendation are identical:

Those wishing to engage in fieldwork or an internship in a country other than Japan after submission of Application.

Interpreting the Requirement

During your studies in Japan, you must not participate in an internship or conduct field research in any other country.

In Book 7 of this series, we will cover your requirements as a MEXT scholar in Japan in detail. One of those requirements is that you must be physically present at your university once per month to prove that you are still there with a student residence status and sign to receive your scholarship. If you do not sign during a particular month, you will not receive the scholarship stipend for that month. If you fail to sign for three months in a row, you lose the scholarship entirely.

When you apply for the scholarship, make sure that your research is to be conducted entirely in Japan and that it does not require any fieldwork or internship to be conducted outside of Japan, and you will be fine!

Post-Doctoral Research Only

The Requirement

The requirements for the Embassy Recommendation and University Recommendation are identical:

Those who have completed a Doctoral course and have no

intention to obtain a degree.

Interpreting the Requirement

If you have completed a Doctoral degree program already, you cannot apply to come to Japan as a research student. You must apply for another Doctoral degree program.

End of the Disqualification Criteria

This concludes the list of disqualification criteria.

Remember, disqualification criteria were listed in such a way that you *must not* meet any of the criteria if you are to be eligible.

For all of the remaining criteria, you *must* meet the criteria to be eligible.

FIELD OF STUDY

The Requirement

There are significant differences between the wording of the requirements for the Embassy Recommendation and the University Recommendation, but as we will cover below, *most* of the same requirements apply.

Here is the requirement from the Embassy Recommendation guidelines for 2019:

Applicants should apply for the field of study they majored in at university or its related field. Moreover, the fields of study must be subjects which applicants will be able to study and research in graduate courses at Japanese universities.

The fields of study may be restricted to particular fields by the Japanese Embassy/Consulate General (hereinafter referred to as the "Japanese diplomatic mission") in the applicant's country.

Traditional entertainment arts such as Kabuki and classical Japanese dances, or subjects that require practical training in specific technologies or techniques at factories or companies are not included in the fields of study under this scholarship program.

A student who studies medicine, dentistry or welfare science will not be allowed to engage in clinical training such as medical care and operative surgery until he/she obtains a relevant license from the Minister of Health, Labor and Welfare under applicable Japanese laws.

Here is the requirement from the University Recommendation guidelines for 2018:

Applicants should apply for the field of study they majored in at university or its related field. Moreover, the fields of study must be subjects which applicants will be able to study and research in graduate courses at the nominating university.*
*My translation.

As you can see, there are far more detailed requirements under the Embassy Recommendation guidelines, but this is because applicants' universities are not yet determined. MEXT expects that almost everything included in the embassy requirements would also be evaluated by the university, prior to your selection.

Interpreting the Requirement

There are so many different elements rolled up in here that it is easy to get lost. Let's take it step by step.

1. You must apply in a field that you have previously majored in at university or a related field.

Confused? You are not alone. I have answered more

questions on this requirement than perhaps any other aspect of eligibility.

If you are applying in a field that was your major upon graduation from a previous university, at the undergraduate or graduate level, you will be fine. If you double-majored, you can apply in either field. If you focused on a particular field in a non-degree program, such as a graduate certificate, that may be acceptable, but since there is no clear rule, it would be subject to the embassy or university's discretion. That means you need to have your justification in order!

If you changed your major part-way through your degree, then the pre-change major would not count.

Majors are straightforward. Here's the tricky part: What counts as a related field? Depending on whether you are in social sciences/arts/humanities or STEM, you could see more or less flexibility. Interdisciplinary majors (like Area Studies) would have the easiest time because they would be able to choose any of the fields they covered under the umbrella of the interdisciplinary major.

In either the social sciences or STEM side, sub-fields, or fields that cover similar contents are a natural "related field." For example, if you majored in political science in undergraduate and wanted to study international relations in graduate school under the MEXT scholarship, that would obviously be acceptable. International relations is a subset of political science and there is significant overlap. The same would go from changing from mechanical engineering to robotics.

But what about more drastic changes? It all comes down to your ability to justify it.

If you can make the case that your undergraduate degree in political science (yes, I keep coming back to this) led you to research micro-finance of entrepreneurial ventures in developing countries as a means of establishing political stability, you could conceivably relate that to applying for an MBA focused on those same kinds of enterprises.

Even if your fields are even more distant, it is still possible if you make the case.

An applicant whose undergraduate degree was in neurobiology once asked me if it would be possible to switch to graphic design. Those seem pretty distant, and I have no expertise in either one, but with a heavy dose of creativity, it might just be possible.

If that applicant had done research into recovery from brain trauma and had discovered that certain visual patterns could stimulate the development of new neural pathways in the brain, then perhaps the applicant could have spun that into a justification into studying graphic design with that specific context in mind. (However, even in that case, it may make more sense for the applicant to apply in neurobiology.)

If you are trying to make a far-fetched connection, then brainstorm ideas early and go over them with colleagues from each field. If you are still enrolled in your previous degree, start brainstorming transition pathways early, so that you can steer your research for the rest of your studies and further justify the transition.

2. The field of study must be available at Japanese universities in a language you speak.

Before you decide on your field of study and start writing your field of study and research program plan, you should identify the university (or up to three universities for the Embassy Recommendation) that you want to apply to and the professor(s) you want to study under.

You need to make sure that your field of study is taught in a graduate program at a university and that it is available in a language you are qualified to study in. You can find out from universities' websites which degree programs are taught in English, so this should be fairly simple to follow.

There is one key exception: For fields of study that focus on Japan: Japanese literature, Japanese history, Japanese linguistics, Japanese law, etc., you will only be eligible to study in a Japanese-taught program under the MEXT scholarship, even if there are English-taught programs available. For any of those fields, assume you would need N1-level Japanese ability, but contact the universities in advance to be sure.

If you are only able to find programs taught in Japanese, or you are studying one of the Japanese-taught fields above, you will need to be fluent in Japanese, even if there are faculty members there who speak English. All of your classes and assignments, including your thesis or dissertation, would be in Japanese. If you find yourself in that situation, research what level of Japanese language ability is required for self-financed international student applicants to apply to that program and ensure that you meet or exceed that requirement.

As long as you have researched target universities and found at least one degree program taught in English that you want to apply to, you will meet this part of the requirement.

Of course, you would need to have that information in hand before completing an application for the University Recommendation, but it applies equally to the Embassy Recommendation. I have heard from applicants in the past who applied for the Embassy Recommendation in the field of Medicine, but were rejected because there were no English-taught programs available and they had no Japanese ability.

Here are three sites that list Japanese universities that teach degree programs in English. I recommend you search there!

- JASSO: List of Universities with degrees taught in English: http://www.transenzjapan.com/jasso/
- JPSS: List of Universities with degrees taught in English: http://www.transenzjapan.com/jpss/
- Univ in Japan: Lists of English-Taught Degree Programs: http://www.transenzjapan.com/univ/

3. For medical or dental programs that require a practicum, you would need to be fluent in Japanese in order to obtain the licenses required to practice or participate in a residency.

In those cases, the scholarship would also only cover the three years required to earn your academic doctorate. You would not be able to extend it for a residency period after those three years, even if that is required to earn a license to practice.

4. Programs that are specifically not covered, like Kabuki from the Embassy Recommendation requirement, are generally subjects that are not taught in graduate programs at Japanese universities, anyway.

These fields are more appropriate to colleges of technology or specialized training, which are not covered by the MEXT scholarship for research students.

The reference to Japanese traditional performing arts being excluded means that you cannot train to become a performer under this scholarship. This distinction is more clear in the original Japanese version of the requirement. You would still be eligible to enroll in an academic program that researches performing arts, just as you would in a program that researches literature, etc. Of course, just like literature, this type of program would only be available in Japanese.

Prohibited Fields of Study

In addition to the relatively clear requirements for the field of study, there is a "secret" requirement as well: Certain field of study are prohibited under the MEXT Scholarship. Fortunately, this is a relatively narrow prohibition and easy to avoid.

Like other "secret" eligibility requirements, you will not find this in the eligibility to *apply* for the MEXT scholarship. It is listed in the eligibility requirements for embassies or universities to *recommend* applicants for the scholarship.

You will be allowed to apply, but if your research field falls under the prohibition below, you would simply not be accepted.

The Requirement
(From the requirements for universities to submit nominees to MEXT)

Universities must be familiar with the Japanese government's policy toward research related to the illegal exportation of goods or research that could be related to weapons of mass destruction and must not recommend for the scholarship any students who intend to conduct research in a field of study that could be applied to the development or production of weapons of mass destruction.*
*My translation. (References to the government policy documents mentioned in the eligibility requirement deliberately omitted.)

The references in the original requirement include a 108-page document in Japanese on the export of technology related to weapons of mass destruction. For the sake of brevity, I am not going to translate that here.

Interpreting the Requirement
As long as you are not seeking to conduct research that

could be used for creating biological or chemical weapons, nuclear weapons, or rocketry, you should be fine.

PAST OR PRESENT RESIDENCE IN JAPAN

The Requirement

The requirements for the Embassy Recommendation and University Recommendation are identical:

An applicant shall, in principle, obtain a "Student" visa at the Japanese diplomatic mission located in the applicant's country of nationality, and enter Japan with the residence status of "Student." Accordingly, even if the applicant already has other residence status ("Permanent resident," "Long-term resident," etc.), the applicant must change it to the "Student" status and re-enter Japan. Moreover, the applicant should be aware that after expiration of the status as a MEXT Scholarship student and even if the student again applies for their original resident status of "Permanent resident" or "Long-term resident," the such resident statuses might not be necessarily granted.

Interpreting the Requirement

If you do not have Japanese nationality, are not currently residing in Japan, and have no plans to reside in Japan before enrolling in your MEXT-funded degree, you do not need to be concerned with this requirement.

Even if you have resided in Japan in the past, have visited or will visit Japan as a tourist (Temporary Visitor) or previously held Japanese nationality, that would not pose any risk to your eligibility.

You must also be eligible to apply for and receive a student visa for Japan. In general, this means that there must be no restrictions on your ability to leave your home country and no restrictions on your ability to get a visa to enter Japan. The only reasons that would prevent you from obtaining a visa to enter Japan are a history of deportation from Japan (or departure on a Departure Order) or being an internationally-wanted criminal or terrorist.

Current Residence in Japan

If you currently hold a residence status for Japan or are a Japanese citizen, you will need to prove that you will surrender that status in order to be eligible to apply for a student visa.

If you are a dual national and have Japanese citizenship, you must prove that you will surrender your Japanese citizenship before starting your scholarship.

The most difficult situation is applicants who are still living in Japan at the time of application. There are two general categories of applicants in Japan: Those already pursuing a degree in Japan with a Student residence status, and those living in Japan on any other status.

For applicants who are currently enrolled in a degree program or non-degree program at a Japanese university with a Student residence status, you will need to prove at the time of application that you will complete your studies in Japan and return to your home country at least two months prior to the start of the scholarship period. In this case you have to prove that your plan to return home is definite, regardless of the outcome of the scholarship application.

There is no particular standard of proof you must meet, but if you are enrolled in a degree program that ends at least two months before you would enter Japan as a MEXT scholar, that would be sufficient.

For applicants residing in Japan on any other residence status (such as Permanent Resident, Long-term Resident,

Dependent, Spouse of Japanese National, etc.), there is no particular timeline for when you would have to return to your home country. However, you can assume that the two-month guideline (or more) will apply to you, too. In any case, you would need to apply for your student visa at the Japanese embassy in your home country at least two months before the start of your scholarship.

Just like Student residence status holders, you would have to provide convincing proof that you have plans to leave Japan and surrender your current residence status regardless of the outcome of the scholarship. This can be rather more difficult to show for other statuses.

When I processed MEXT scholarship applications for a Japanese university, I ran across this situation at least a few times each year. Often, I saw applications from spouses of current students at the university who were living in Japan on Dependent residence statuses. We would ask them to submit a written explanation of their plans to leave Japan and return to their home country, including the dates and reasons why. (Of course, we never followed through to check if unsuccessful applicants really stuck to their plans, we just needed to have the applicants' plans on hand to protect ourselves if MEXT came asking.)

GPA

Typically, you will not find the GPA (grades, average marks, weighted average, etc.) requirement listed anywhere in the eligibility criteria, whether you are applying for the Embassy or University Recommendation. However, it is a real requirement.

To be eligible to be nominated for the MEXT scholarship, you must have a minimum of a converted 2.3 GPA on MEXT's unique 3.0 scale. We will go over how to convert your academic performance to this scale below, and you can find sample conversion tables in Appendix A.

The first important thing for you to understand is how GPA is considered in the application process. GPA is a minimum eligibility requirement to *be nominated* for the scholarship, not to *apply*.

What difference does this make? If you do not meet one of the eligibility requirements to apply that we discussed above, then the Embassy or University would not be able to receive your application for review. In that situation, they would have to return your application materials to you and explain why do not meet the eligibility requirements to apply.

It only makes sense to include eligibility criteria that can be evaluated quickly and without a doubt.

Converting every applicant's GPA, grades, marks, weighted average, etc., from the home university's scale to the MEXT scale is a time-consuming process. In many cases, your grades are going to be in sealed envelopes, which could only be opened after the application is officially received. So it is generally not possible to include it in the eligibility criteria.

Here's where it hurts, though: If you meet the eligibility requirements to apply, but not the eligibility requirements to be nominated (GPA), then the university or embassy can receive your application. At the end of the application screening (the document screening, for the embassy), they will simply tell you that you were not selected. In that situation, they do not need to tell you why or return anything to you. You would never know if your GPA was holding you back.

Fortunately, we are going to go over how to calculate your GPA now, so you should know if you are eligible before you even start the application.

Embassy Recommendation: Local Grade Requirements

As we will cover below, embassies in each country are allowed to set their own additional eligibility requirements, as well. Some will choose to set a minimum grade requirement in your home country's system.

In that case, you will have to abide by that requirement separately from MEXT's 2.3 out of 3.0 requirement, even if they are not an exact match.

Calculating Your GPA

You are going to need to get your academic transcript and the TranSenz GPA Spreadsheet I sent you if you downloaded the bonus documents. If you have not gotten those yet, you can grab them now from the link below:

http://www.transenzjapan.com/bonusmms1/

You can also do this with a pencil and calculator, if you enjoy doing things the hard way.

For the sake of simplicity, I am going to use "transcript" to refer to the document or documents that show your academic performance in each of your classes. Depending on your country's or university's system, this document might have a different name, such as "marks sheet". The important thing to remember is that it is the official document, issued by the university, that shows your academic performance for each class you took.

First, let's get clear on what counts for the calculation.

When converting your grades to the 3.0 system, MEXT only includes the grades you earned over your most recent two full years of study in a degree-seeking program, unless you meet one of the following exceptions:

- You transferred schools at the same degree level during the past two years. In that case, only grades earned *after* the transfer would count toward the calculation. (You will still need to turn in the pre-transfer transcript, as well).

- It is not possible to determine which grades fall within the past two years. For example, in universities that only show grades per year, not per semester. In a situation where it is not clear which grades fall within the last two years, they would calculate the last 2.5 years, instead.

- Your last two years included 1 or 3 semesters of graduate school, and your undergraduate program only calculated grades on a year-by-year basis. In that case, the most recent 2.5 years of grades would count (as in the example above).

- For the most recent two years of study, you have been enrolled in a program that does not issue any grades, such as a research-only Master's degree program. In that case, your Letter of Recommendation from the Dean (or higher) of your last university would have to show explicitly that you were in the top 30% of your class at the university or faculty level.
  (Note: If your GPA can be calculated and is less than 2.3, then a letter saying that you were in the top 30% would not make you eligible. It only works if you have no grades available whatsoever).

The following grades will not be counted:

- Grades such as "pass" in a pass/fail course are not counted. Grades of "fail" in a pass/fail class should not be counted if it is evident from your transcript that the class was pass/fail. They will be counted if it is not obvious that the course was pass/fail. Some universities may include them, anyway, so if you have any grades that meet that criteria, include them in the calculation, just in case, to see the worst-case scenario.

- Grades earned in a class that awarded zero credits or zero graduation credits.

- Caveat to the previous bullet: If your university shows failed courses as being worth zero credits on your transcript, those grades would still count. And the number of credits for GPA calculation would be equal to the number that you would have earned if you had passed.

- You studied abroad during the past two years and your study abroad grades transferred back to your home university as pass/fail grades. In that case, those grades would not count and that semester (or semesters) would not count toward the two years. Even though you will likely have to turn in the transcript from your study abroad, if the grades are not reflected on the transcript of the university you graduated from, they are not counted.

Grades earned during summer sessions or other inter-semester sessions that fall within the last two years, will be counted, but the summer session, etc., will not count toward determining the two-year period of time. A summer or other short session that falls before the first semester or year counted would not be included.

How to Calculate Your GPA on the MEXT Scale

You will need to determine what scale to use to convert your grades from your university's scale to MEXT's 3.0 system. The charts in Appendix A show several sample conversions, along with images of the original grading system taken from the transcripts. Find the one that best matches your grading system.

The TranSenz GPA Spreadsheet: Entering the Conversion Table

If you cannot find a sample grading system in the appendix that matches yours, send me a scan of the front and back of your transcript by email to travis@transenzjapan.com with the subject line "Grading Scale Check" and I will find a match for you or create a new scale based on your transcript and add it this book's bonus materials.

If you are using the TranSenz GPA Spreadsheet, enter your conversions in the conversion table section. You will need to enter every grade available on your system on the left and the converted MEXT grade on the right. Here's an example based on a system with grades A-D and F, where plus and minus grades are both considered subsets of the letter grade.

Conversion Table	
A+	3
A	3
A-	3
B+	3
B	3
B-	3
C+	2
C	2
C-	2
D+	1
D	1
D-	1
F	0

If you have a grade that you are not sure how to convert (for example, I have seen universities use the grade "B/C") then I recommend converting it to the lower possible score. Your calculation is not going to be final and official. You are only doing this now to make sure that you meet the minimum requirement, so be harsh on yourself.

Entering the Grades

Next, simply enter the grade you earned and the course weight in each line of the Grade Table. Your converted GPA will calculate automatically. You do not need to enter the course titles, unless you want to do so for your own reference.

Course weight means how much the course counts toward your graduation.

In some university systems (including Japan), you have have to acquire a certain number of credits in order to graduate. In that case, your course weight is the credit value of the course. If your university requires you to acquire a certain number of marks to graduate and uses weighted marks, then your course weight would be the maximum number of marks available in that course.

If your university only requires that you complete a certain number of courses and does not weight any course more than another, then your course weight for each course would be "1".

Here's an example of entering the grades into the Grade Table. You only have to enter the grades in your home system. The sheet will do all the calculations for you.

Grade Table		
Course Name	**Local Grade**	**Weight**
Course 1	A+	3
Course 2	B	3
Course 3	C	3
Course 4	B+	3
Course 5	A	3
Course 6	A-	6
Course 7	B+	3
Course 8	B	3

Calculating Your GPA by Hand

If you are not using the TranSenz GPA Spreadsheet (why not?) you can do the same calculation by hand with a calculator and pencil. I recommend making a photocopy of your transcript and writing directly on that.

Once you have your conversion scale, as we discussed above, convert each grade, one-by-one, to the equivalent grade on MEXT's scale. Then multiply the MEXT scale by the course weight to get the point value for the course. You cannot convert your overall average, as that will give you an inaccurate result. (See the sample calculations in Appendix A for an illustration of why this is the case.)

Add up all of the point values and all of the course weights, then divide the total point value by the total weight value to get your result. Here's how it would look with the 8 courses I listed above:

Grade Table				
Course Name	Local Grade	Weight	MEXT Grade	Point Value
Course 1	A+	3	3	9
Course 2	B	3	3	9
Course 3	C	3	2	6
Course 4	B+	3	3	9
Course 5	A	3	3	9
Course 6	A-	6	3	18
Course 7	B+	3	3	9
Course 8	B	3	3	9
Total		27		78
GPA	(Total Point Value / Total Weight)	(78/27)		2.88

For the final result, you drop any numbers beyond the second decimal point. Do not round!

If you do the calculation above yourself, you will see that the answer is 2.88888888. . . This does not become 2.89, it stays 2.88. At that score, it does not really make a difference, but if your GPA calculated out to 2.2988888888 instead, then you could not round it to 2.30 (eligible), it would stay 2.29 (ineligible).

EMBASSY-IMPOSED ADDITIONAL REQUIREMENTS

If you are applying for the Embassy Recommendation, there may be additional eligibility requirements.

Each Japanese embassy, in consultation with your country's local government, is allowed to impose additional eligibility restrictions. For example, they may demand that you meet a minimum GPA in your home country's scale or they may limit the scholarship to specific fields of study.

Since this is decided on a country-by-country basis, the only way to find out if there are additional requirements for your country is to check with the local Japanese embassy or consulate, directly.

Universities are also allowed to impose additional eligibility criteria, both for the Embassy Recommendation and the University Recommendation. In my experience, however, the only restrictions they tend to add are language proficiency requirements, particularly for programs taught in Japanese.

ELIGIBILITY - CONCLUSION

That wraps up the list of eligibility criteria. Here's the moment of truth: How did you do?

If you have just been reading through so far, and have not stopped to review the criteria, use the worksheet on the next page, or the one in the downloadable bonus documents and do a self-review, now. There's no sense in moving on until you have made sure you can.

If you meet all of the criteria we have reviewed, congratulations! There is nothing standing between you and winning the scholarship, as long as you are willing to put in the work. We will start with that in the next chapter, as we discuss your application strategy.

On the other hand, if you did not meet all of the eligibility criteria, I am sorry to hear that. Unfortunately, that does happen. At least you know now, before spending countless hours on your application, not to mention money for tests and postage. You can focus on other opportunities instead. I wish you the best of luck!

EXERCISE 3: ELIGIBILITY

Answering the questions below will help you ensure that you are eligible for the scholarship and clear up any doubts or questions you might have about eligibility.

As before, you can fill out your answers in a notebook or download the exercise worksheets that go with the book at:

http://www.transenzjapan.com/bonusmms1/

1. What is the last degree you earned? Or, if you are still enrolled in a degree program, what level is that degree and when will you finish all of your graduation requirements? Level: / Completion Date:

2. Have you earned, or will you earn, the prerequisite degree before arriving in Japan (Earned a Bachelor's degree for Master's applicants or a Master's degree for Doctoral applicants)? Yes / No

Your answer to question 2 must be "yes" to be eligible.

3. Do you have Japanese nationality? No / Yes

3.a. If yes, are you a dual national and willing to surrender your Japanese nationality? Yes / No

If you answered "yes" to question 3 and "no" to question 3.a., you are not eligible to apply. Any other combination of answers is eligible.

4. Does your country of nationality have diplomatic relations with Japan? Yes / No

If no, you are not eligible to apply.

5. What year are you applying?

5.a. What year will you start your studies in Japan?

5.b. Subtract 35 from 5.a.

5.c. Is your birth date on or after April 2 of the year you calculated in 5.b.? Yes / No

If you answered "no", and you do not meet the exception requirements described in the age section, you are not eligible.

6. Do you have language proficiency test scores for the language you plan to study in? Yes / No

6.a. If not, and you are not a native speaker, when is the next TOEFL iBT/IELTS/JLPT test in your area?

Reference:

- TOEFL iBT Test Dates and Locations:
  http://www.transenzjapan.com/toefl/
- IELTS Test Dates and Locations:
  http://www.transenzjapan.com/ielts/
- JLPT Test Dates and Locations:
  http://www.transenzjapan.com/jlpt/

7. In what ways could you leverage your research to contribute to the local community (e.g. giving presentations or lessons to community groups, working on specific projects)?

8. Are you willing to get involved in visits to schools and public organizations or volunteer at festivals and events while in Japan? Yes / No

9. Are you currently an active-duty member of the military or a civilian employed by the military? No / Yes

9.a. If you answered yes to question 9, are you able to be discharged or released from your contract before you would start your studies in Japan? Yes / No

You must have answered "no" to question 9 or "yes" to question 9.a. to be eligible.

10. Is there any reason (work, school, inability to obtain passport) that you would be unable to leave your home country during the time specified by MEXT to arrive in Japan? No / Yes

You must have answered "no" to question 10 to be eligible.

11. Have you ever been deported from Japan or left Japan under a Departure Order in the past? No / Yes

11.a. If you answered "yes" to question 11, you will have a specific period during which you are not permitted to reenter Japan. When does that period end?

11.b. Would your studies start after that date? Yes / No

You must have answered "no" to question 11 *or* "yes" to question 11.b to be eligible.

12. Have you received a MEXT scholarship (other than the Japanese Studies Scholarship, the Japan-Korea Joint Government Scholarship Program For The Students In Science and Engineering Departments, or the Young Leaders Program) in the past? No / Yes

12.a. If you answered "yes" to question 12, what was the last month when you received a scholarship payment?

12.b. How many months of university enrollment or employment as a faculty member or researcher do you have since that date, starting with the month after your last payment?

You must have answered "no" to question 12 or "36" or higher to question 12.b to be eligible.

13. (University Recommendation, only) Do you plan to apply to only one university per year via the University Recommendation process? Yes / No

You must have answered "yes" to question 13.

14. Are you currently enrolled in a university in Japan with a "Student" residence status? No / Yes

14.a. If you answered "yes" to question 14, will you graduate and return to your home country before the start of the degree program that you are applying to via the MEXT scholarship? Yes / No

You must have answered "no" to question 14 or "yes" to question 14.a to be eligible.

15. Do you plan to enroll in a Japanese university as a self-financed student between the time you apply for the MEXT scholarship and when you arrive in Japan to start your scholarship-funded studies? No / Yes

15.a. If you answered "yes" to question 15, can you prove that your program will end and that you will return to your home country at least two months before the start of your scholarship program?

You must have answered "no" to question 15 or "yes" to question 15.a to be eligible.

16. Are you applying for or have you been selected for any other scholarships that will provide money for tuition, living expenses, etc., during your time as a MEXT scholar? No / Yes

If you answered "yes" for question 16, you must be prepared to cancel your application or withdraw from the award for any other scholarships. (But not for grants for specific projects, etc.)

17. Does your research plan require you to conduct field research or participate in an internship outside of Japan? No / Yes

You must have answered "no" to question 17 to be eligible.

18. If you have a Doctoral degree already, are you applying for a Doctoral degree program under the MEXT scholarship? Yes / No

You must have answered "yes" to question 18 to be eligible.

19. Describe how your intended field of study in Japan is directly related to your major or to research you have already conducted at university.

20. Write the name of at least one university in Japan that teaches your field of study at the degree level you want in a language you are qualified to speak. You can find programs taught in English at any of the sites below:

- JASSO: List of Universities with degrees taught in English: http://www.transenzjapan.com/jasso/
- JPSS: List of Universities with degrees taught in English: http://www.transenzjapan.com/jpss/
- Univ in Japan: Lists of English-Taught Degree Programs: http://www.transenzjapan.com/univ/

21. Do you plan to pursue a professional degree in medicine or dentistry? No / Yes

Unless you are fluent in Japanese (native level), your answer to question 21 must be "no" to be eligible.

22. Does your research concern materials or technology that could conceivably be used for the development or production of weapons of mass destruction? No / Yes

Your answer to question 22 must be "no" to be eligible.

23. Are you currently residing in Japan with a residence status other than "Temporary Visitor"? No / Yes

23.a. If you answered Yes to question 23, prepare an explanation of exactly when and why you plan to leave Japan and surrender your current residence status. One paragraph to half a page should be sufficient.

24. Calculate your GPA using the TranSenz GPA Spreadsheet (or by hand). You can download the spreadsheet from:

http://www.transenzjapan.com/bonusmms1/

What is your GPA (maximum 2 decimal places)?

Your answer to question 24 must be 2.30 or higher.

CHAPTER FOUR:
Your Application Strategy

Now that you understand the MEXT scholarship and benefits and have confirmed that you are eligible, it is time to plan your application strategy.

It is not enough to simply be a good student and have a great research idea. That might get you the scholarship and it might not. I do not know about you, but "might" is not good enough for me.

Actually, I think I do know about you. You bought a book about improving your chances of winning the scholarship. So, I'm assuming you also do not want to settle for "might" and want to take every possible step to increase your chances of winning the scholarship

As we discussed in the chapter on the successful applicant mindset, you need to approach the application process as a professional. A professional does not leave anything to chance. A professional learns everything he or she can about the challenge ahead and takes steps to prepare.

Applying for the MEXT scholarship is like a soccer match or sumo tournament. If you want to win, you need to know the rules of the game, you need a good coach to get you ready, and you and your coach need a plan of attack that will help you maximize the benefits of your strengths and control the flow of the game to ensure your victory.

I'm here to be your coach, so let's get started with your game plan.

YOUR THEME: HOW YOU WILL SERVE

The first step in any game plan is deciding what outcome you want. In other words, your goal. If you do not have a goal, then you do not know what you are working toward and any effort you make might be in the wrong direction.

Let's get one thing out of the way:

Your goal is not to win the MEXT scholarship. Your goal is *what comes after.*

Ultimately, Japan does not award the MEXT scholarship just to fund students or degrees. The Japanese government wants to identify and support applicants who have the best chance of making a positive impact in the world - in line with the Japanese government's own objectives, of course - and becoming leaders in their communities. Japan wants these leaders and innovators in countries around the world to be connected back to Japan, both through personal relationships, and through a sense of appreciation.

If that tarnishes your image of what you thought was a purely academic effort, good. That's an important step in understanding your strategy. You need to know what the Japanese government wants.

Fortunately for you, what the Japanese government essentially wants is outstanding global citizens who have a connection to Japan. If you are applying for a graduate degree in Japan, then that's what you want to become, whether you realized it before, or not.

So, what is your goal?

Let's start with your theme.

The core of your MEXT scholarship application strategy, which we will call your application theme, is deciding what difference you want to make in the world. Keep it to a single sentence, to start.

How do you want to serve the world?

Do you want to contribute to peace between nations? To

alleviating poverty? To food security? To education? To environmental sustainability? To promoting understanding between cultures?

Your theme does not have to be obviously related to your field of research. I know a young woman who majored in photography, but her theme for serving the world was marine conservation. She once told me she regretted not majoring in something like marine biology. But as a photographer with a passion in that area, she could do things for marine conservation that a biologist might not be able to do, like raise awareness through emotional photojournalism and building a movement. Do not trap yourself with false limitations.

Once you have your theme, write it down. Use the exercise at the end of this chapter or the downloadable worksheets. There is something powerful about putting themes and goals down on paper. It will take you much closer to reaching your goal than simply keeping it in your head. I'm going to ask you to write your theme at the top of nearly every paper related to your strategy and, later, related to your Field of Study and Research Program Plan. (Yes, we might sound like we are getting a little off topic for now, but trust me, this will all connect!)

If you have multiple ways you want to serve the world (I know I do) and cannot decide. Write them all down, first. Then choose the one that resonates most with you right now. The wonderful thing about service is that once you start down that path, you will continue to find new and exciting ways to contribute to making the world around you a better place. You will always have the opportunity to come back to your other ideas in the future.

If you really, really can not decide, you can move forward with two ideas for now, and decide during the next stages where you want to focus. You do need to decide eventually, though. Many things will change during your application process and study. Your goals might shift, your professor in Japan could steer you to a different research subject, you might find a whole new area of research that excites you. That's all fine. But once you decide your theme, how you want to serve the world, that should not change.

Next, we are going to work on taking that general theme and working it breaking it down into specific actions and results.

GOING FROM THEME TO GOAL: Goal Brainstorm

Once you have decided on your theme, it is time to brainstorm as many specific ways to contribute to your theme as possible.

You can make a list (there is space in the worksheet for this), draw a web that branches out from general to specific, attack a whiteboard with a marker, whatever works best for you in getting as many ideas as possible out of your head and into writing. Remember, writing is powerful.

Do not censor yourself at this stage or reject any ideas. Write them all out as they come to you. You never know when something that might sound stupid could be the seed of another, better idea. Keep them all as visual cues.

Stop and spend at least 10 minutes, or more, if you can, to do this before reading ahead. Keep going until you run out of ideas, then force yourself to come up with five more. Often, it is only after we think that we have exhausted every possible avenue that our brains get creative and come up with the best concepts.

Next, we are going to review how to narrow down your list, but I do not want you thinking about that process yet and unintentionally limiting your brainstorming.

Narrowing Down Your List

You have your brainstorm list, right?

Good. Because now it is time to start whittling that list down to something that you can use to steer your application.

I recommend making a copy of your list to work on. As you eliminate ideas, cross them out, but do not obliterate them. You may want to go back to them or build on them later.

The first thing you want to do is eliminate anything that you can accomplish right now, without going on to graduate school. This goal is going to have to connect to your research. If it is something you can already accomplish, then you could start working on that right away instead of going to graduate school, first.

Graduate school is about conducting independent, original research. It is not about applying existing research, except for some cases in engineering fields. You should be looking at goals that you do not yet have the required knowledge to pursue.

Next, you want to look for goals that are out of your control, require resources that you can not get access to (yet), or are ideas that you would not be able to start working on for more than five years after your graduation. Do **not** eliminate these goals. Instead, try to create an interim goal that will help you on the way to each one; find something that is within your power and is something you can start tackling within five years of graduation.

Do not underestimate yourself!

For example, if you had a goal to establish a human colony on Mars, that's probably not something you can reasonably pull off within five years with your resources, unless you happen to be Elon Musk. But it would be a reasonable goal to develop a self-contained mini-farm that could help sustain the growth of plants on Mars.

If you want to restructure tertiary education in your home country to encourage innovation instead of rote learning, that could take a while to accomplish single-handedly. But your interim goal could be to become a professor at a university in your home country to start that pedagogy change on a grass-roots level and present on your results at academic conferences to start influencing the change.

Figure out what works best for you and your goals!

Relating to Your Studies

While you are thinking of interim goals - or if you are using one of your brainstormed goals, directly - look for ways to relate the practical goal to what you have studied in the past. The Mars example above works if you have a research background in bioengineering, but what if you have the same goal and a background in literature? In that case, you would be able to contribute to the establishment of a Mars colony by identifying common themes in space colonization literature across cultures so that you could use the results of your research to inspire public awareness and enthusiasm for colonizing Mars.

If you cannot find any way to relate one of the goals on your list to your past research experience, then eliminate it for now. You can always come back if you figure it out later.

Results

Hopefully, by now, you have three to five goals remaining that excite you, are related to your past research and future goals, and are reasonable achievable within five years of graduation. Write them down on a separate list.

VALIDATING AND REVISING YOUR GOAL IDEAS

Now that you have several ideas of goals that serve your application theme, it is time to validate and revise.

The clearer and more focused you are on your goal, the better you will be able to narrow down your research question for your Field of Study and Research Program Plan. You will have an easier time selecting what university or universities to apply to, since you know your ultimate goal. And you will come across as more focused, confident, and promising throughout your application process.

Before we get started on your goal, let's look at what makes "bad" goals. A "bad" goal is not necessarily a goal to do something bad. You do not need to be Ernst Stavro Blofeld or Lord Voldemort to have bad goals.

A bad goal is unfocused, vague, or short-sighted. It does not give you enough information or guidance to move forward and make decisions.

Once we have gone through a few bad goals, we will look at the SMART goal-setting framework and make sure that your final goal statement for your application meets that framework.

What Makes a Bad Goal

There are many ways to write a bad goal, but the most common I see among MEXT applicants is this one:

They never look any further than winning the scholarship.

I have people write me to say that they want the MEXT scholarship because the quality of education in Japan is better, so they will be able to contribute more to their society after graduation.

No good.

Others write that they want to increase their chances of employment.

No good.

Some applicants really respect Japanese culture and want to spend more time surrounded by and experiencing that culture on a daily basis.

No good.

All of these goals are focused only on the applicants' personal gain, and all would be accomplished simply by winning the scholarship. These goals show no promise for the future or indication that the applicant will ever contribute to the world in a meaningful enough way to validate the Japanese government's investment.

Another way you can go wrong is by being too vague.

I have had applicants write to say that they want the MEXT scholarship so that they can contribute to world peace.

Sorry, but your winning the scholarship does not make the world a more peaceful place. This "goal" fails because it is too vague and there is no clear path. As I mentioned above, contributing to peace between nations can be a theme, but it is not specific enough to be a goal.

Another, well-meaning but ultimately deficient goal is: I want to contribute to my home country.

How? There is no specificity here, either.

As you set your goals, you want to make sure that they serve others and that they meet the SMART goals framework that we will discuss next.

Goals with a History of Success

Remember that your application theme should be about service to others. There are a few common goals that are specifically related to service, are considered desirable outcomes by MEXT, and have a history of success, particularly among applicants from developing countries:

- Becoming a professor to disseminate the knowledge you obtained in Japan to future generations.
- Becoming a government employee with responsibility over policy decisions, where you will be able to use your knowledge and experience in Japan.

It is not enough just to say that you want to become a professor or public servant. You will still need to come up with a specific field of research that you want to spread in your home country, along with a reason, or a specific field of policy that you want to tackle. But these are both tried and true goals that can help you shape an application.

Even if you do not want to become a professor or a bureaucrat, there are endless possibilities for success, so do not be discouraged.

You can find successful applicants from the past who have shared their research proposals and, more importantly, their thinking and planning behind them. Adopting their research ideas wholesale is never a good idea, but understanding their thought process and what went into their planning can help you create strong goals and a winning field of study and research program plan. I will introduce some of these samples in Book 2 of this series.

SMART Goals

Now that you understand what to avoid, and a few clear paths, it is time to focus on how to write goals that will drive you toward success. These are the kinds of goals that will give focus to your research plan, help you come across as being confident and competent, and set you apart from unfocused applicants.

The best goal-setting framework I know of is SMART goals. This is the system that successful entrepreneurs and business coaches use. I know this is a scholarship application, not a business. That's fine. The goal structure has nothing to do with business and everything to do with success. It is just that businesses, and particularly entrepreneurs, are the most success-driven people, so that is who we want to emulate.

As you have probably guessed, SMART goals is an acronym. For now, we are going to go through what each letter means and how it is relevant to you. You do not need to create your goal from start to finish yet. We will do that in the next few sections and in the worksheet. For now, it is important just to understand the final objective.

- **S - Specific:** What exactly do you want to achieve? Where? When? How? Why? The more details you know about your goal, the stronger your focus and the easier it will be to achieve, since you will not get lost or confused. (We have already covered the "why" with your application theme, so you have a head start!)

- **M - Measurable:** How will you be able to tell if you are making progress toward your goal or achieve it? Since we are talking about a goal that you want to achieve after graduation, and so much might change before then, it may seem difficult to commit to a specific measurement. But you do need to think about how you will be able to measure your goals.

- **A - Attainable:** Do you have the resources, or the ability to obtain the resources, to achieve your goal? Is it possible within a set amount of time? Most importantly, are you willing to make the personal sacrifices necessary to achieve it? This is a significant difference between your application theme, which is a cause you want to contribute to, and your goal, which should be a concrete, attainable outcome. You want to push yourself - remember, if your goal is something you can already achieve now, then you will not be able to use it to justify your scholarship application - but do not break yourself or set yourself up for failure.

- **R - Relevant:** Is achieving this goal something that is important to you, personally. Is it something you really want, or something you think others want from you? I have found with my work with students over the years that many who break down during their studies are ones that are following their parents' dreams, not their own. Their dad is a doctor and pushed them to follow the same path, or their career counselor pushed them to go into computer programming for the money. These students, though many were brilliant, struggled and often changed direction, losing time and money. Make sure your goals are relevant to what you want for yourself.

- **T - Time-bound:** Parkinson's Law states that work expands or contracts to fit the time allowed. If you set yourself a goal but do not put a deadline on it, you will lose focus, slow down progress, and risk never completing it. For your application goal, I recommend setting a goal that you plan to achieve within five years. This might impact what you consider "attainable" during that time, so these two criteria need to go hand-in-hand. Of course, when you write your Field of Study and Research Program Plan, you will need a specific timeline for your research goals, too, so this is great practice!

I realize all of that can sound a little overwhelming as we get started. You have not even started your studies yet. It is ridiculous to be setting a goal for 5 years later, based on the assumption that your studies will go as planned.

Yes, that is true. The goal you set know will inevitably change. So will your research plan. That's fine.

The point of writing goals now is not to commit absolutely to achieving them. The point is to give you direction and focus in creating your application and to show the application reviewers that you are capable of setting goals and pursing them on your own. Displaying that skill for the sake of the application process is more important now than the actual goals.

For now, let's figure out a goal that appeals to you and will help you in the process of choosing your research question and selecting universities in Japan.

CRAFTING YOUR GOALS

The SMART goal framework is written in an easy-to-remember order, but it does not always make sense to tackle the elements in that order. If you already have a strong focus, then you can address each letter in the order that you prefer. But most people who come to me asking for advice have not even yet decided what they want to study, so we are going to start from that assumption.

We will start with R: Relevant. In this first step, we will make sure your goal ideas from the earlier brainstorm list are important to you, personally, and something you are motivated to achieve.

Next, we will revisit T: Time-bound. We have touched on this before with the five-year assumption, but we will get more clear on your specific situation.

Next, we will move on to S: Specific. You will decide on something specific that you want to achieve within the five years, including the what, where, and how. (We have already nailed when and why with the previous steps!)

This is most likely going to be the most significant and most challenging step, so it is OK if this takes you a little time to get through.

Once you have your specific goal, you will make sure it is A: Attainable. Finally, you will come up with ways that it could be M: Measurable.

As always, the worksheet is here to help you along the way and the good news is that you have two letters nearly complete!

Relevant:
How do Your Studies Serve Your Purpose

Look back at your application theme. Is this truly something that *you* want to do? Make sure your theme is not something that others have forced on you or pressured you into accepting. Hopefully, by this time, that is not a problem.

Now, look at the rough goals that you brainstormed earlier. You probably still have a few left on this list at this point. Focusing on relevance to what you want for yourself in life, choose the one that is most valuable and exciting to you.

This might sound a little selfish, but if you wrote all of your goals out of a position of how you can best serve the world around you, then there is nothing selfish about choosing between different ways to serve. In any life of service, it is critically important that your goals be relevant and personal to you. Your internal motivation to pursue your goals will help you get through challenges even when the rest of the world does not seem to care.

Any successful service must be supported be a personal, intrinsic desire or passion to see it through for your own benefit. This is not selfishness, it is essential to your success.

Go back to your list and circle the goal that you are most passionate about.

Now, write one to two sentences describing why you are passionate about achieving this goal. When you write your Field of Study and Research Program Plan and when you participate in the interviews, you will need to be able to explain why your research and post-research goals are important to you. So, these few sentences are a first draft of an explanation that you will actually use in your application!

Now, you should have your application theme, a rough goal, and a statement of why achieving that goal is important to you!

It is time to put some clear definitions on that goal.

Time-Bound:
A Clear End Point

As I mentioned earlier, we are going to assume a five-year period after graduation, so T - Time-bound is practically already taken care of. Of course, you may have goals that are longer term and grander than what you can achieve in five years. That's great! But even five years (plus your study time) is a long way out and plenty can change in that time. We will work on setting a SMART goal in that five year period that will serve your longer-term goals.

That will also help you articulate to the MEXT scholarship reviewers how you plan to make an immediate impact.

If you are concerned with five years being too long and potential changes, remember this is not set in stone. The purpose of this goal is to shape your application strategy, not to commit you to a result.

Take a minute, too, to ensure that your schedule is realistic. If your goal involves sequential steps, make sure you have allotted enough time for each step. Consider setting a Time-Bound deadline for each of the sequential steps you need to make toward your goal!

Specific:
Going From Rough Goal to Defined

Going from a rough goal to a specific one might take some time. I do not recommend that you sit down and try to solve this all at once. You might need to go for a walk or sleep on it partway through.

You will probably come back to revise this step again as we continue to develop your application strategy. You do not need to get it perfect on the first go around. We will validate the specifics as we consider the Attainable and Measurable criteria. We will also likely need to reshape your goal when we "MEXTify" it in the next section to connect it to specific research and to Japan.

Consider this your "Specific" first draft. You can always change these details later, but first you need to have something to build on.

At this point, you have your application theme, which is how you want to serve the world. You have a list of several goals that serve that theme, including one that you have circled as the most meaningful, or Relevant, to you. You have also established why that goal is important to you.

Now, we are going to give that goal some shape. We are going to answer:

- **What** outcome you want to achieve as a result of your studies in Japan.
- **Where** you will take action and achieve this outcome.
- **When** you will plan to achieve the outcome.
- **How** you will achieve the outcome.
- **Why** this outcome serves your application theme.

Let's break down each of those questions.

What

When answering "what" you want to achieve, this should be an outcome that you have the power to accomplish. It should not be dependent on outside feedback or appraisal that you cannot control.

For example, I once worked on rural rehabilitation projects in a war zone in southeast Afghanistan. One of our missions was to improve the availability of education. So, we had a specific goal to construct at least one boys' school and one girls' school in each of the major towns of our province. Our "what" was to build the schools. That was under our control. We did not set a goal to have a certain number of female students attending the school, for example, because we could not force parents to send their daughters to school.

If we had based our goal on getting a certain number of students, that would have been beyond our control, so it would not have been good enough for a SMART goal.

Your outcome should be within your control, even if you need help to achieve it. If you want to introduce a new technology, then your goal could be to create a proof of concept, but you should not set a goal based on adoption rates. If you want to go into government service and affect policy decisions, then your goal should be to write and lobby for proposals, not to guarantee their implementation.

Adoption rates (or school attendance rates, in my case) can and should be goals that you go after later, but remember your time constraints and focus on outcomes that are related to your research, for now. Developing a proof of concept is a technological task and one that would be appropriate for a science or engineering degree. Encouraging adoption is a marketing task and would be better related to an MBA.

Where

Where are you going to have your impact?

In general, MEXT wants to see you working in your home country. The idea is that graduates return to their home countries to become a bridge between that country and Japan and to strengthen relations.

However, maybe your goal requires that you be working in Japan to develop a specific technology or political initiative that will help your home country and strengthen relations. That could be possible, but the impact area is still your home country, in that case.

Of course, your impact area could be more narrowly defined. Maybe you are interested in urban planning and disaster preparedness for a specific city, for land management in a specific national park, or to become a professor at a specific university. Those are all valid "where"s, as well!

When

Earlier, I encouraged you to set your goal within five years of completing your degree. That is for the sake of focus. A task that will take you more than five years is likely to be based on multiple cross-supporting initiatives. I wanted you to choose one.

But you do not have to stick to five years as your target. If your goal will or should take less time, be specific about it. Consider how you might have to work with calendar events. Is your goal related to seasons of the year? Is there a specific deadline?

How

How are you going to achieve the outcome you specified under "what"?

You do not need to go into too much detail here - this is only a goal statement, not a complete plan - but you need to be clear about the general activity you need to complete to achieve your outcome.

Why

This statement links your "what" to your application theme. What greater purpose does your outcome serve?

You should already know this, but be sure to include it in your statement.

Example

Taking my schools example above, here is a statement that covers all aspects of the "Specific" criteria:

I will construct one boys' school and one girls' school in the city of Qalat, Afghanistan, in time for the start of the 2022 school year, in cooperation with local officials and construction companies and with financing from USAID, to enable a higher education level among the next generation of citizens and improve the functioning of government and civil society.

Breaking this down, here are the elements:

- What: Build one boys' school and one girls' school
- Where: In the city of Qalat, Afghanistan

- When: In time for the start of the 2022 school year
- How: In cooperation with local officials and construction companies and with financing from USAID
- Why: To enable a higher education level among the next generation of citizens and improve the functioning of government and civil society

The point of this example is to show a complete goal statement. In addition to being specific, this goals statement is also Measurable (two schools), Attainable (assuming I was still working in rural rehabilitation in Afghanistan), Relevant (there are few things more important to me, personally, than contributing to the availability of education opportunities), and Time-Bound (2022 school year).

Of course, this specific example is not a good proposal for the MEXT scholarship, because nothing about this goal requires further research. We will look into shaping goal statements to be appropriate for the MEXT scholarship a little later on.

Attainable: Reality Check

Look back at your goal statement that we wrote in the "Specific" section and decide: Is this really something possible?

You should have written what you want to accomplish and how. If you need collaboration, especially funding or cooperation, is it within your means to obtain? Is your goal something that world conditions allow?

Using the worksheet, write out what you need from other people to achieve your goal, and how you plan to get it.

My sample goal of building schools was Attainable for me when I was working in Afghanistan, because I was part of a NATO team and had access to all of the people and resources I need. Now, it would not be Attainable because I am no longer part of that world.

You should also consider obstacles that might make your goal Attainable. Is there potential political resistance to your idea? Are there physical obstacles, if your goal involves working in remote or difficult areas? Does your goal rely on technology that is not commonly available or not affordable?

For each obstacle you consider, write out a way to overcome it, or modify your goal to avoid the obstacle.

Your goal should be ambitious, but if you are not confident that it is even possible to attain, then consider scaling it back. You can always set a new goal once you have hit the first!

For the purposes of the MEXT scholarship, you may also have to defend the Attainability of your goal during the interview stage. If you set a goal that is clearly impossible, or if you cannot make a clear argument as to how it would be possible, then scale back to something you can explain. It will not look good to the committee if your goal sounds like an unrealistic pipe dream.

Measurable: Ensuring Quantifiability

If it isn't measured, it isn't done

Your goal should have some form of objective measurement. You need to know when you have met the goal and you also need to be able to track your progress along the way.

In the previous example, my goal was to build two schools. That is something I can easily measure and also something I can track by looking at the construction progress of each school throughout the life of the goal.

Your goal will probably be more difficult to measure. Try to think of ways you can measure your physical output if you are producing either physical products or intellectual products like policy proposals or artworks. If your goal involves developing a new technology, then you can measure your progress toward achieving completion, patenting, production, etc.

Your goal statement is going to be one (long) sentence, so you do not need to go into too much detail, but know what aspect of the goal you will measure and how you will know how close you are to completion.

Your SMART Goal

By now, you should have a SMART goal drafted in your worksheet. Congratulations! That's a great first step.

But you might be looking at your goal and asking yourself, how does this relate to my application for a graduate degree?

Remember, this goal is what you want to accomplish after your degree. So, your studies in Japan must get you to the point where you can start work on attaining this goal. Later, when we discuss your Field of Study and Research Program Plan in Book 2, we will create a separate research goal for your studies.

In the next section, we will walk through the process of making sure that your goal connects directly to a research program to be conducted in Japan.

"MEXTIFYING" YOUR GOAL:

Connecting it to Your Studies in Japan

We have reviewed the SMART Goals framework, which is the best approach to setting clear, attainable goals to push you forward. But that is a general framework. In order to make sure that your goals are appropriate for the MEXT scholarship application, we have a few more steps.

In the next sections, we are going to make sure that your goal is related to graduate studies, that it is connected to Japan, and that it strengthens connections between Japan and your home country.

Research Connection

For your goal to be relevant to the MEXT Scholarship application, it *must* require you to conduct original research.

If you already have all of the knowledge you need to get working on your goal, then you cannot use it as justification to apply for a graduate degree. You must need some additional knowledge to be able to complete your goal.

This knowledge can be anything from a more detailed mastery of specific techniques or technologies, a deeper understanding of case studies and examples than what is currently available, or new research into present conditions.

Remember, all graduate degrees in Japan are research degrees. There is no such thing as a "taught Master's", where you just take courses and absorb information. You will be expected to research primary sources to draw new conclusions, conduct experiments, and/or conduct your own field research (in Japan). One of those activities, and its results, must be necessary to your goal.

Here are a few examples:

If you are in humanities and social sciences, consider how research of primary sources in Japan can help you develop the knowledge you need to tackle a problem. For example, researching a particular event in Japanese history to apply a greater understanding of the relationship between contemporary conditions and individuals actions to the outcome to a similar decision point or problem in your home country.

Social science and humanities scholars should also consider how fieldwork in Japan can connect to their goal. Can studying Japanese society through surveys, interviews, etc., help you better understand a particular social issue (such as aging society) to implement social programs in your home country?

In sciences and engineering, your goal statement should be dependent on the development of new technology and systems or the adaptation of technology/systems to conditions in your home country.

Fine arts scholars' goals should require studying directly from Japanese Master's in their fields to merge the understanding of their techniques and philosophies with previous knowledge to create new branches in arts.

How does this apply to you? Write out what research, new knowledge, or new abilities you require to achieve your goals. If your goal statement does not require any new research or understanding, then you should consider either forgoing the MEXT scholarship to get started on your goal right away or revising that goal statement to establish a clear need for research before you can start.

Why is Japan the Best Place for Your Studies?

During the application process, you will need to establish a connection between your goal and Japan.

Simply saying that you want to study in Japan because you grew up addicted to manga and anime is not going to impress the review committee, unless your research is directly related to those art forms. So, you will need a stronger reason.

There are several proven reasons that will establish the connection beyond a doubt. Associating one of these with your goal and your research will give you a stronger case for why your research must be conducted in Japan. These are listed in no particular order. Any of them would be solid reasons.

- You want to conduct field research on a specific incident, case study, or region of Japan to apply that knowledge to your home country.

- Cutting edge research in your field is being conducted in Japan.

- Japan - or even better, a particular university - offers access to unique research resources, such as a particular lab or experiment.

- You have already established a relationship with a professor in Japan based on your research and want to continue to work with them.

- Japan has a unique perspective on your field of study that you cannot explore elsewhere.

- Your post-graduation goal involves working with Japanese

companies or organizations in your home country (such as JICA development projects).

- There is a compelling reason why you need to establish a research network with Japanese universities or professors that you will continue to leverage, and offer benefit to, after graduation.

As a few of these examples suggest, you do not necessarily have to focus on Japan as a whole. If you can make a case why your research must be conducted at *a specific university in Japan*, that is even stronger for our purposes. Remember, the point of your goal statement is to give you a clear focus, so that you can wrap your entire application around a central theme and impress the reviewers with your organization and preparation. Clearer is better.

You want to avoid selfish or short-sighted reasons, such as "because Japan offers a generous scholarship." Even seemingly flattering reasons like saying that you respect Japanese culture and society and want to experience it is not going to be compelling unless you can connect that experience to your specific goal. It is in your best interest to have a practical connection between your goal and research and Japan.

Even if you had not thought of any of these reasons when starting your application strategy, work one into your plan now. This might require revising your specific goal to take into account a field of study where Japan is more advanced. It may also require looking for an example of a case study in Japan that you can apply to your goal.

Even if it takes some time, it is worth the effort to make your application appear that much more organized and focused!

How Does Your Goal Serve the Relationship Between Japan and Your Home Country

In addition to thinking about why your research must be conducted in Japan, you need to have an idea about how it will benefit Japan.

The goal of the MEXT Scholarship, from the Japanese government's perspective, is to create connections between rising leaders in countries around the world and Japan. They want you to go home, contribute to your society, and share how Japan helped you get to the point where you could make that contribution.

If you are applying for Embassy Recommendation, then it is likely that your review committee will include local academics or government bureaucrats from your home country, as well. These people will also have a vested interest in how you will return to help develop your home country and strengthen the connection with Japan.

In many cases, it is enough to say that you will leverage the knowledge and experience you gained in Japan to directly benefit your home country through your efforts and that you will actively advocate for others in your field to study in Japan or work with Japan in the future. Sharing what you learned or experienced in Japan will appeal to the review committee.

This approach works especially well if you plan to go into teaching, but can also work in any practical development field or government service.

Maintaining research relationships with Japan after returning home and exchanging knowledge with your connections in Japan is also a strong connection. It is one of

MEXT's explicit goals for the scholarship to expand research networks of Japanese universities overseas.

Remember, too, that one of the unmeasurable eligibility criteria is that you must be willing to participate in follow-up surveys and events conducted by the Japanese Embassy in your home country to promote Japanese culture. If your research is directly related to Japanese culture, such as in humanities fields, then you could propose that you will spread that knowledge through seminars, exhibitions, or events. You will want to be more specific, as appropriate for your field, of course.

Even in other fields, including technical fields, proposing to give presentations at local universities or schools, which could inspire more interest in studies or research collaboration in Japan, would also be beneficial.

If you can connect any of those activities to the promotion of your goal, that is excellent.

In the worst case scenario, even if there is no obvious direct connection to the attainment of your goal, you should at least be prepared to explain how you plan to advocate for study in Japan to others in your field in order to strengthen human capital in that area, which will further multiply the results of your efforts.

Your SMART Goal, MEXTified

At this point, you should have established a SMART goal that has a clear relationship to Japan.

That puts you ahead of the vast majority of applicants for the scholarship! If you get nothing else out of this book - even if you do not read any other books in this series - you already have a tremendous advantage.

As you complete each of your MEXT application documents and prepare for your interview, keep this goal statement in front of you at all times. When you are considering what to say, whether to include something or not, or how to explain a particular experience or motivation, relate it back to this goal.

If you do this, you will come across as being organized, reliable, focused, and a strong candidate for the scholarship. The reviewers will see you as someone who can fulfill their objectives after graduation and contribute to Japan and the world.

This is a huge step, but we are not finished.

Your scholarship application does not exist in a vacuum. It is not just a matter of being "good enough" to earn the scholarship. This is a competition. And like any competition, you need to know the rules as well as what you are up against.

As the next part of preparing your application strategy, we will look at those rules and try to gain a better understanding of the "opposition" and obstacles you may face, as well as how you can prepare to overcome them.

THINK ABOUT YOUR "OPPOSITION"

"If you know your enemy and know yourself, then in a thousand battles you need not fear defeat."
– Sun Tzu

Yes, I am aware that Sun Tzu is not Japanese. But this quote is relevant to any endeavor, even if it is too often misinterpreted.

The misinterpretation is usually based on the word "enemy." If I say "enemy" to you in the context of the MEXT scholarship application, you might assume I mean the other applicants who are competing for the same scholarship places.

But that's not what I mean.

I prefer the word "opposition." Opposition is less negative and more clearly refers to anything that resists your efforts to achieve your goal. An enemy is someone you fight against; opposition is something you overcome.

For the MEXT scholarship, other applicants are not your only opposition. Your opposition includes the application process itself as well as the embassy- and university-level reviewers. You will go head-to-head with the application process, especially trying to understand the complicated requirements, confusing instructions, and unclear expectations. Your application documents, and you, yourself, will undergo scrutiny by reviewers who are looking to eliminate candidates.

This is your opposition and what you need to understand.

Fortunately, you have this book, plus Books 2 through 5 in this series, which are designed to help you understand and excel in the key stages of the application process.

As you plan your application strategy, you need to consider the application process from the perspective of the reviewers. Before you submit any document, send any email, or participate in an interview, stop and think about the person on the other end. What does that person want? How can you create an outcome that meets that person's wants as well as your own.

Consider What's in it for the Other Person at All Times

The best resource I have ever encountered on understanding other people's wants and persuading them to your point of view is Dale Carnegie's book, *How to Win Friends and Influence People*. I highly recommend the book in general and you can often find the ebook for extremely cheap prices on

Amazon. You can find a link in the resources at the end of this book.

I cannot summarize the entire *How to Win Friends* in these few short paragraphs, but I will highlight some of the most important points.

Your task is to understand what your opposition (MEXT, your reviewers) want and phrase your own goals in such a way that they match what the opposition wants.

MEXT and the Embassy

MEXT wants you to become a leader in your home country and a cultural ambassador for Japan throughout your career. Becoming a leader does not mean that you have to become president. You can be a leader in government service, but you can also be a leader as a professor or administrator in academia, a leader in industry, a leader of a community, or a leader of social or cultural movement.

Of course, it may take more than the five years we set previously to reach a leadership position, but your first goal should be a concrete step along that path.

From that position of leadership, as small or large as it may be, consider how you can be an ambassador for Japanese culture. We covered this earlier, but it bears reiterating, when you state your post-MEXT studies goal in the Field of Study and Research Program Plan and describe it in your interview, you should make every effort to connect it to your role as an informal ambassador for Japan and contributor to relationships between Japan and your home country.

Your Government

If your government is involved in the selection process during the Embassy Recommendation, you will need to place emphasis on how your goal serves your people or your home country in a meaningful way.

Your Desired Adviser in Japan

When you start building a relationship with your desired advising professor in Japan, you should follow the basic tenets of any networking effort: Offer value.

Unlike the embassy and government staff, who may be concerned more with what you will do after graduation, university professors in Japan will be more interested in your research goals and how that could offer value to the professor's own research and field of study.

You should learn all you can about your professor's current research and initiatives before contacting him or her and describe your own research goals in relationship to how they compliment your adviser's

In science and engineering fields, you will often have to work on a specific research project that your professor needs done, especially at the Doctoral level.

In humanities and arts (fine and liberal), you may not be working directly on a sub-theme of your professor's research, but you will be helping to broaden the scope of research within their field.

Of course, in any field, a goal to publish and/or go on into academia yourself also benefits your adviser by increasing his or her stature in the field.

You do not need to be obsequious or volunteer yourself as a professor's slave. I would recommend you stay away from that. Present yourself as someone who desires to become a peer and long-term research connection, and you will put yourself on a path to a stronger long-term relationship.

WHAT WILL HELP AND HURT YOUR CHANCES

One of the most common questions I have seen over the years on my blog has been "Will X help my chances to win the scholarship?" Or the opposite, "Will Y hurt my chances to win the scholarship?"

Applicants ask if past experience studying abroad in Japan will help them, or if never having left their country will hurt them. Will some Japanese language ability help? What about being a research assistant or the president of a university manga club?

After reading the last several sections, you may already realize what is wrong with these questions.

Other applicants have more practical, but still misguided questions, like asking whether applying for the same level degree that they have already earned will hurt them.

You will hear this answer *a lot* once you win the scholarship and arrive in Japan: It depends.

The problem with the questions above is that they refer only to isolated facts. They are missing the "so what?" factor that gives them significance. Over the last several sections of this book, we have gone over goals and building your application around a central theme. Facts are not going to help or hurt you unless you give them meaning and connect them to your goal.

The right question to ask is: "*How* can I use X to help my chances to win the scholarship?"

Over the next few sections we look at the kinds of experiences and abilities that can be helpful, help you find examples in your own life, and, most importantly, figure out how you can leverage those facts for maximum benefit to your application.

What Are Your Superpowers

You have superpowers.

I do not mean that you can fly, read minds, or shoot laser beams out of your nose.

I mean that there is *something* you do better than most people around you. There is some unique experience, background, passion, or combination that you bring to the table that no other applicant does. We have to identify what that is.

You do not have to be the best in the world at whatever your superpower is. Chances are good that your superpower is really a combination of things: A particular background, plus experience, plus passion in a field, plus an ability. That combination - your story - makes you unique and you can use that uniqueness as an advantage.

What Are You Good At?

I've said this before, but it bears repeating: I know only one thing about you for sure. I know you are the type of person who invests in yourself and your goals. You didn't just approach the MEXT scholarship application with the attitude of "Well, I'll give it a shot and hope it works out." You bought a book to study the application process and how to make your application stronger. Chances are, you have also combed through all of the free advice and information I've posted on my blog as well. Right?

So, I know you are the kind of person who has a thirst for knowledge and makes the effort to understand their tasks and goals.

I'm also going to assume that you are the kind of person who puts in the work to make those goals a reality. You have been filling in the worksheets as we went along, right?

That right there is a significant superpower. You take steps on your own to learn what you need to succeed in your goals and follow through with action to make it a reality. You may take it for granted because it's a trait you possess, but trust me, it is rarer than you think.

So, that's one superpower. It's your turn to come up with more:

- What do you do better than most people around you? (Do not overlook "mundane" abilities like clear communication, time management, or analytical ability!)
- What do other people come to you for help with?
- What are you so passionate about that you would do it all day, even if you were not getting paid?
- When you work in a group, what task to you usually take on?

(All of these questions are on the worksheet, so you can fill in your answers there to keep them all together!)

If you are modest or self-effacing, you will fit in well in Japanese society, but you might struggle to complete this list. In that case, ask friends and family what *they* think you are good at and write those things down, as well.

Do not leave anything out, even if it seems irrelevant. Even skills that are not directly relevant to your goal or your research in Japan may be based on a more fundamental ability that you can apply. By listing everything out, you will be able to find common themes and make connections that you would not have realized if you were self-censoring.

For example, I am an excellent baker. My friends and

family go crazy for my sweets and breads. That does not necessarily sounds like it could be connected to a research goal, but it is. My skill in baking is based on my ability and dedication to study the recipe, prepare my workspace in advance, measure precisely, implement the correct mixing techniques, and practice practice practice until I get my creations right. Those are all skills that I could apply to research in Japan, even if I never brought a cake into the lab.

Once you have your list of skills, do what I did with the baking example above and extract the relevant parts. Look for characteristics that show up across multiple superpowers. For example, in baking, I mentioned studying the recipe in advance. I have several other superpowers where my success is based on my ability to analyze the task and be completely prepared in advance, so that is something I would want to connect to my research goal.

Strength of Past Accomplishments

To paraphrase *Hamlet*, there is nothing good or bad, but framing makes it so.

When you list your past accomplishments, you must put them in context. Do not expect your reviewer to make that connection. Do not expect your reviewer to understand why a particular achievement or experience makes you a stronger candidate for the scholarship.

Whenever you mention your past, whether in the Field of Study and Research Program Plan, during the interview, or in communication with your prospective adviser, make sure to link it to your goals and your understanding of the reviewer's needs.

Some accomplishments have obvious connections, but even in these cases, you should still mention the obvious, even if briefly. Remember, your reviewers are probably seeing dozens of applicants. They are probably hearing the same things over and over. You need to make your statements stand out by highlighting them with characteristics and results that the reviewers are looking for.

For example, earning high grades is great. But explaining how you earned those grades, or the lengths you were willing to go to when you struggled and needed to work extra hard, will help show your dedication and will persuade the reviewers that you will be able to overcome the transition to a higher-level degree in a new country.

If you have worked as a research assistant, do not just state the fact, explain that it gave you experience in the operation of an academic lab and ongoing research as well as how it contributed to your passion to further your own studies.

If you have studied abroad in the past, whether in Japan or another country, simply stating that will not help you as much as explaining how you grew and how you will apply that experience to your studies in Japan. If you do have study abroad experience, remember that in addition to your goal and your "opposition's" needs, the reviewers also want to make sure that you can adapt to life in Japan. Leverage this experience to show how you adapted to a new culture and academic system, got involved in the community, and how you will apply that to your MEXT studies.

Use your past achievements and experiences to highlight your unique characteristics and advantages to the review committee and you will gain a significant advantage over the applicants who simply list up their past and expect someone else to make the connection.

Language Proficiency and Professional Certifications

Besides proficiency in the language of your degree program, which is obviously required, you can leverage other language proficiencies or professional proficiencies related to your field of study.

High proficiency in a particular language, at the native level, for example, gives you access to a broader research network and resources. If you can find a way to connect that potential to your research topic, that is another superpower you can leverage in your application.

Even low levels of language proficiency can give you a small advantage. Having a little proficiency in other languages can tell the review committee that you are the kind of person who likes to learn about new languages and cultures and makes the extra effort to communicate and get involved. Those are highly desirable traits for MEXT scholars.

Of course, as we just discussed, you need to make sure that you are drawing that deliberate connection. Do not leave it to the review committee to figure it out on their own.

For professional certifications, you only need to focus on qualifications that are relevant to your goal or studies. Honestly, over the course of three years and well over 500 applications, I never once saw an applicant submit a relevant or useful certification. So, if you do not have one, it is not something you need to worry about.

I used to see applicants submit passing certificates for introductory courses in Microsoft Office use. Nobody cares. That's about as valuable as a certificate saying you have learned how to brush your teeth.

On the other hand, if you have a certification or license related to your field of study that you had to work for, that is absolutely something you should bring up. For instance, if you have a veterinary license and are applying for a PhD in life sciences to research animal pathogens, your background is relevant. If you have passed the LEED exam for green architecture, that would be relevant to an architecture or urban planning degree.

If you have an advanced professional certificate that is *not* related to your field of study, then once again, its value comes down to how well you frame it. You will need to find a way to connect that certification to how it has led to your current research interest. If you can show that connection and explain the transition in fields, then you can use that example to prove your dedication to excellence in whatever field you pursue.

If you cannot find a way to connect your past certifications to your current interest, and you are afraid that it will look like you are disorganized or change your mind rapidly on a whim, you may want to leave those out of your application altogether.

If you do not have any professional certifications, do not worry. It is not going to put you at any significant disadvantage. But if you do, that is one more tool you can leverage, so try to find the best way to connect your certifications with the goal of your studies!

Japan Experience

Any experience with visiting Japan, interacting with Japanese people, or taking part in Japanese cultural activities is something that you can leverage for the benefit of your application.

There are three primary ways you can leverage your experience with Japan:

1. Prove to the review committee that you will be able to adjust to life in Japan
2. Show why you are motivated to complete your research in Japan
3. Highlight relationships in Japan to show your preparedness and focus

Ability to Adjust to Life in Japan

Particularly in the interview, your reviewers are going to want to determine whether or not you will be able to adjust to life as a graduate scholar in Japan, away from your culture and your support network of family and friends. This is where you can use your experience to ease their concerns and quickly check that box off of their review criteria.

If you have lived in Japan for any length of time, that is a great thing to mention. Alternatively, experience working with Japanese citizens or exchange students in your home country to help them adjust to life there is also valuable, since it offers an example of how you have already come to understand the cultural differences and helped people to overcome them in the opposite direction.

Experience studying Japanese culture or being part of a Japanese cultural group can also be a useful leverage point. If you participated in tea ceremony, for example, you could talk about how you plan to continue to take part in that once you arrive in Japan and use that experience to build your local connections and adjust. It also shows that you have some experience as a cultural ambassador already.

If your only experience with Japan is growing up watching anime and reading manga, mention it, but I would not suggest that you go into much detail, unless you are specifically researching one of those media. Your reviewers may be wary that you will face culture shock when you learn that Japan is nothing like its portrayal in anime or that you have false expectations about the country.

If you do bring up an anime or manga interest, I would recommend that you refer more to the artistic styles and your interest in the underlying themes, rather than the content.

It is important to mention that when you leverage your past experience with Japan to show that you will be able to adjust to life in Japan, you are only trying to check off a box. Keep your reference to your experience in Japan short and simple. Use the strongest connection you have to answer their question and keep moving. Stay focused on your goal and your application theme.

Why You Are Motivated to Research in Japan

Earlier, we established why your research had to be completed in Japan. Mentioning past experience with Japan or Japanese culture and how that kick-started your interest in your research topic is one way to reinforce that point to your reviewers, show your motivation, and establish a grounding point in Japan.

Preparedness and Focus

If you have study abroad experience at a Japanese university and remain in contact with your faculty members there, that is something you can leverage separately when you establish your dedication to your research plan. Showing that you are already in contact with faculty members in Japan about your research and have interest from a professor is going to be a strong mark in your favor.

We will cover building relationships with faculty members in Book 3 of this series, but remember that a relationship built in person while in Japan serves both your research and proof of your preparedness to live in Japan!

Potential Obstacles and Disadvantages

I mentioned at the start of this section that applicants often contact me to ask whether a particular condition or situation will hurt their application. The most common questions I get fall in to the three categories below:

- Applying for the same level of degree that you have already earned in the past
- Long periods of unemployment
- Lack of any intercultural experience

Remember what I said earlier: Asking if something will help or hurt you is the wrong question. If you have any situation that you are concerned might hurt your application, the question you need to ask is, "How can I keep this from hurting my application chances?"

The answer is that you need to justify the situation by connecting it to your goal and application theme. Do not just make excuses for yourself, phrase your explanation as a reason why the potential obstacle actively contributes to your goal.

I will cover the three topics above in more detail, but you can use the same justification approach for any potential obstacle or weakness.

Repeating a Degree

If you have already earned a Master's degree, for example, and want to apply for another Master's degree in Japan, you need to justify that decision.

Why is a second Master's degree more advantageous to your goal than a PhD would be? What does a Master's degree offer you that a Doctoral degree does not?

I have never seen an applicant offer a satisfactory answer to this question when continuing in the same field of study. In general, if you are continuing in the same field of study, then there should be nothing a second Master's offers that a Doctoral degree would not. The only possible justification I can see is a pivot. If you had earned an MSc and focused on developing a new technology in your research and now want to learn techniques to better distribute that technology, then it could make sense to transition to an MBA. Or perhaps to a field like urban planning or policy science where you could study implementation of your new technology.

I would not recommend that you try to justify repeating a degree by saying that you are not academically prepared to move on to the next level. That does not make you look good.

There is one practical consideration to keep in mind, as well. If you are applying to repeat a degree that you have already earned, you would *not* be allowed to start as a research student. You would have to start directly as a degree-seeking student.

Unemployment or Gaps in Your Work/Academic History

Gaps in your academic and work history can look bad on paper, even if there is a perfectly legitimate reason for it. Japan is a society where many of the older generation still attach high importance to belonging to an organization. In fact, if someone is mentioned on the news, whether for good or bad reasons, their employer (or lack of employment) will almost always be stated. A high proportion of criminal suspects are identified as being unemployed, so there may be an unconscious bias against that status.

I'm not necessarily saying that is the right attitude to have, but you should understand that it is a common attitude among the reviewers and be prepared. If your academic and work history shows long periods of unemployment, be prepared to explain those in your interview.

Unemployment because you could not find work is not going to look good. But unemployment because you had to focus on supporting your family at home, or because you were conducting self-study or attempting to become an entrepreneur or independent artist are not bad things. You can highlight those employment gaps for the strengths they represent: desire to serve those around you, constant drive to better yourself, independence, and initiative.

In any of those cases, be prepared to talk about what you did during that period of unemployment and how it motivated your current study interest and goal.

Lack of Intercultural Experience

It is not uncommon for MEXT scholarship applicants to come from poor or remote areas where they have had minimal contact with people from other cultures. There are even regions of Japan where most locals have not had any contact with outsiders. Many applicants have asked me in the past whether it will hurt their application chances if they do not have any intercultural experience.

No. I think that even in this situation, you can find an example of a way you have interacted with another "culture" or way of thinking. If you came from a remote, closed area, then even going to university, for example, would be a form of culture shock. Even if all of your classmates were from the same country, they would have been from other regions. Your professors would have different perspectives from your family and friends at home. Talking about how you adjusted to that new university culture, and how you used that experience to learn how to adjust to new ways of thinking, can help you overcome the absence of any international experience.

Your Application Strategy: Concluded

It's been a long chapter, with a lot of hard thinking and strategizing. But if you have made it this far, you already have a significant advantage over other MEXT applicants.

You have an application theme, a way to serve the world in the future.

You have a SMART goal that serves that theme, which you will use as the focus of your research plan and interview preparation.

You have connected your SMART goal to a research outcome.

You have justified why your research must be done in Japan.

You have thought through what your reviewers want from you as a MEXT scholar and determined how to phrase your goal so that it meets what they want and expect.

You have listed out your superpowers and experiences that you can use to show why you are a better candidate for the scholarship than anyone else.

Finally, you have considered problems and obstacles that could hold you back and come up with a deliberate plan to overcome them.

That's a ton of work to put in, and I congratulate you on making it through. Now that you have this strategy document in place, keep it in view at all times throughout your application. Print out the the Theme and Goal Declaration page from the worksheets and post it on your wall. Refer to it before you fill in any form, write any email, and prepare for your interview. This focus and strategy will guide you whenever you are concerned about what to do next!

As we say in Japan, *gokurosama deshita* (Thank you for your hard work)!

EXERCISE 4: YOUR APPLICATION STRATEGY

The exercises that accompany this chapter are some of the most important in this entire series of books. These questions will help you create your application strategy, from start to finish, and give you a goal-centered approach to the scholarship.

Once you have finished this section, I recommend that you print out your answers and post them over your desk, or somewhere else where you can see them every time you sit down to work on your application – especially the Theme and Goal Declaration.

If you are going to be printing these out, then I recommend downloading the document pack if you have not already done so:

http://www.transenzjapan.com/bonusmms1/

OK, let's get started.

Developing Your Goal

1. In what way do you want to serve the world (What is your application theme)?

2. Brainstorm specific things you could do that would contribute to that theme.

3. Narrow down your brainstorm list to goals that you can reasonably accomplish within 5 years that are related to your research background. List your top 3-5 goals, in order of preference.

SMART Goals

4. After reading the section on Relevance, circle the goal

from question 3 that you are most passionate about, for your own benefit.

5. In one to two sentences, explain why achieving your goal is important to you personally. What is in it for you?

6. What exact outcome to you plan to achieve?

7. Where will your outcome's area of impact be?

8. When will you achieve this outcome?

9. How will you go about achieving the outcome?

10. Why does this outcome support your application theme?

11. Write a draft sentence that incorporates the answers to question 6 - 10 in a single goal statement.

12. If your goal requires any sequential steps, write out each step and the deadline for that step to ensure that you meet your overall completion deadline.

13. What external support (funding, cooperation, permission, etc.) does your goal require?

14. For each support you listed in question 13, describe how you plan to secure it, or if it is impossible to secure, write an alternative final goal that will not require that support.

15. What obstacles do you face in your goal? Consider physical, technological, political, and personal obstacles.

16. For each obstacle in question 15, write how you will overcome or avoid it.

17. What specific aspect of your goal will you measure to determine when it is complete (or how close it is to being complete?

18. If you had to modify your end goal because of obstacles or reliance on outside support, rewrite your goal statement with the new final objective.

Why Your Goal Requires Study in Japan

19. How does your goal require additional, original research?

20. If you cannot identify a clear relationship between the need for research and your goal, rewrite your goal statement so that it does require research, knowledge, understanding, or technology that you do not yet have access to but can acquire during your time in Japan.

21. Why does your research have to be conducted in Japan, or at a particular university in Japan?

22. List all of the ways you can think of that your efforts to attain your post graduation goal could strengthen the relationship between your home country and Japan.

23. List any supporting activities related to your goal that you could do to promote connections between your home country and Japan after graduation.

Considering Your Opposition's Needs

24. How can attaining your goal lead to you becoming a leader in your home country, so that you can be an effective cultural ambassador for Japan? Include the field where you plan to become a leader.

25. (Especially if you are applying for the Embassy Recommendation) How does your goal serve your home country?

26. What value does your research plan offer to a potential adviser in Japan?

Your Superpowers

27. What do you do better than most people around you?

28. What do other people come to you for help with?

29. What are you so passionate about that you would do it all day, even if you were not getting paid?

30. When you work in a group, what task to you usually take on?

31. Ask your friends or family what they think you are good at and write those down, too.

32. What are the common underlying abilities that support each of your superpowers?

Leveraging Your Past

33. What academic experiences do you have (high grades, study abroad, research assistantship, publications, presentations, etc.)? List each experience and at least one way that you can connect that experience to your goal for your MEXT scholarship or to one of your superpowers that will give you an advantage over other applicants.

34. List the languages other than Japanese or English where you have any proficiency and your level (academic, daily conversation, minimal).

34.a. For any academic-level proficiency, how can you use that to serve your research interest in Japan? Are there particular advantages that language offers?

34.b. For daily conversation or minimal proficiency, how can you use that ability to show your adaptability to new cultures and/or willingness to interact?

35. List any professional certifications you have related to your field of study and connect them to your specific research.

36. List any professional certifications you have that are *not* related to your field of study. Note any ways you can leverage them to show your dedication and follow-through ability or connect them to your goal in Japan.

37. What experience do you have with Japanese culture or working with Japanese people? For each one, list the experience as well as one or two ways that having that experience makes you better prepared to adjust to life in Japan.

38. What, if any, disadvantages or obstacles might hold back your application? For each one, list a justification that connects to your goal.

IN CLOSING

We have come a long way together over the course of this short book. Regardless of how well you understood the MEXT scholarship when you started, you should now be in a position to start your successful scholarship application.

We started with an overview of the MEXT scholarship to help you understand what was possible as well as the purpose of the scholarship, from the Japanese point of view. The first chapter provided the information you need to decide on which scholarship application process to pursue, when to start, and how to apply.

In the next chapter, we discussed the mindset you need for success. I introduced the idea of approaching the scholarship application like a professional, as well as the attitude you need to succeed. That seemingly small change in perspective will help you see the scholarship application process in a new light and can help you with difficult decisions throughout the application process.

Next, we went through the long eligibility checklist. While this chapter might have been boring, it should have cleared up any doubts you had about whether or not you could apply. That's important, because if you are *eligible* to apply, then there is no reason why you cannot succeed with the proper mindset and strategy.

Creating your application strategy was the final, and most significant chapter, of the book. It is one of the most overlooked but important steps of the application. Your strategy will guide your application decisions, help you express yourself more clearly and to the point, and give you a huge advantage over applicants who just put their information out there and hope for the best.

Hopefully, you have downloaded the exercise worksheets and followed along with all of the questions as we went through. If you have not, I highly recommend that you do that now!

http://www.transenzjapan.com/bonusmms1/

If you have the mindset and your strategy down, then there is no obstacle that you cannot overcome. You will be able to find an answer to any question you might have. You will know to look for advice when you need it, instead of floundering around.

You have invested in yourself by completing the tasks in this book. Carry that attitude forward and there is nothing you cannot do.

What comes next?

By now, you should know how to approach the application and whether you will start with the Embassy Recommendation or University Recommendation. The application timeline will determine your next step. If the application guidelines are available now, you should get started with the application process. If not, then I recommend that you focus on writing your Field of Study and Research Program Plan and researching universities and advisers in Japan while you wait.

Field of Study and Research Program Plan

In this book, we covered your overall application strategy and your goals for after graduation. Your research must connect to and serve those goals. The most important tool you have to establish that connection - indeed the single most important document in your application package - is your Field of Study and Research Program Plan.

Writing a concise, effective plan that exceeds the reviewers' expectations is critical to your success. You only have a few pages to make an impression, but this document is so critical, that I recommend you give yourself weeks or months to complete and revise it, then seek feedback to make it better.

If you are interested in learning more about how to narrow down your research field, create and validate a research question, and write the final plan, I cover all of those subjects in detail in Book 2 of the Mastering the MEXT Scholarship series:

How to Write a Scholarship-Winning Field of Study and Research Program Plan

Coming Soon! Check the link below to find it at your favorite online bookseller.
http://www.transenzjapan.com/mms2/

ABOUT THE AUTHOR

Travis Senzaki was an international student in Japan, once upon a time, and it changed his life. He is now a university administrator in Japan and works with international students on a daily basis.

He spent three years working as the first point of contact and reviewer of all MEXT scholarship applications at a major Japanese private university, where he personally reviewed over 500 Embassy Recommendation and University Recommendation applications and answered thousands of questions.

Since moving to another university in Japan to work with exchange students, he launched a series of articles about the MEXT scholarship on his blog, TranSenz, and has helped thousands more scholarship applicants through that site. His goal is to help dedicated and able scholarship applicants overcome confusion about the application process, reduce the role of chance in their success, and realize their dreams of studying in Japan.

He continues to follow the most recent news and application developments on the MEXT scholarship, as well as within Japanese higher education, in English and Japanese, and share that information with as many people as he can.

Travis did not know a thing about Japan before arriving here as a high school student, but thanks to amazing host families, he fell in love with the country's history and culture. Eventually, he moved back to Japan with his wife shortly after the Great Northeast Japan Earthquake.

He is a permanent resident of Japan and lives in Akita with his wife and three children.

Other Books by Travis

Travis writes practical manuals for living in Japan as well as epic fantasy novels.

Mastering the MEXT Scholarship Series

Available now or coming soon!

1. **How to Apply for the MEXT Scholarship**
   http://www.transenzjapan.com/mms1/
2. **How to Write a Scholarship-Winning Field of Study and Research Program Plan**
   http://www.transenzjapan.com/mms2/
3. **How to Find your best Degree Program and Adviser for the MEXT Scholarship**
   http://www.transenzjapan.com/mms3/
4. **MEXT Scholarship: The Embassy Recommendation Application Process**
   http://www.transenzjapan.com/mms4/
5. **MEXT Scholarship: The University Recommendation Application Process**
   http://www.transenzjapan.com/mms5/
6. **Preparing to Move to Japan: A Handbook for MEXT Scholarship Winners**
   http://www.transenzjapan.com/mms6/
7. **MEXT Scholar and Beyond: Life in Japan**
   http://www.transenzjapan.com/mms7/

Other TranSenz Guides

How to Get a Spouse Visa for Japan: The TranSenz Guide
http://books2read.com/spousevisa

Epic Fantasy Novels (as T.A. Senzaki)

Breyik the Apprentice
http://books2read.com/Breyik

EXERCISES

If you have not completed the exercises earlier in the book and want them all in one place, here they are.

As a reminder, you can download these exercises as a worksheet, with space to answer questions, plus a list of all the links and resources in this book from:

http://www.transenzjapan.com/bonusmms1/

Chapter 1: Understanding the MEXT Scholarship
Your Degree

1. What degree do you want to earn by the end of your scholarship? (Master's / PhD / Professional Master's / Professional Doctorate / Research Student only)

2. What is the first degree you need to earn to get there?

3. Do you have a reason that you need to earn your degree quickly and return to your home country (e.g. if you are on a leave of absence from work)?

4. Are you applying to repeat a degree that you have already earned? If so, why?

Your Application Schedule

5. What month is it as you are reading this?

Ideally, you should start preparing for your application up to 6 months or more before the application deadline.
If it is between December to May*, you should consider applying for the Embassy Recommendation first.
If it is between June to November*, you should consider applying for the University Recommendation first.
(*If it is late May or late November, you may not have enough time, check your individual embassy or university for more information)

6. Based on the explanation above, what application process are you going to apply for first? (Embassy / University)

Your Goals and Resources

7. What is your life goal that will be helped by earning the degree you wrote above via the MEXT Scholarship? (It can be a broad goal for now, we will refine it later!)

8. What practical resources do you have that you can use to aid your scholarship application?

☐Contact with your academic adviser from your last degree
☐Contact with a professor in your field in Japan
☐A strong relationship with an academic professional who can review your Field of Study
☐Access to a university library
☐Contact with someone who has won the scholarship in the past
☐Contact with a friend or professional who can proofread your application
☐Other

Chapter 2: Successful Applicant Mindset
Confidence

This is an exercise I still use every time I think I do not have what it takes. It always helps me at least to pretend that I have the confidence I need long enough to get the job done.

1. Are you concerned that you will not be able to compete for the MEXT scholarship?

2. Why? What disadvantages do you think you have? Be specific.

3. Do you think no other applicant has those same problems or concerns?

4. If every other applicant is human, too, with strengths and weaknesses, what strengths do you have that can set you apart from them? (Here's one: You are the kind of person who is willing to invest the time and money in yourself to succeed, as evidenced by the fact that you are reading this book and following through on the exercises!)

5. If you apply for the scholarship and do not get it, what's the worst that could happen to you? Again, be specific.

6. Is that worse than the consequences of not applying?

Professionalism

7. Imagine *you* were offering an award worth 10,000,000 yen. How would you expect applicants to address you?

8. What characteristics would you look for in their plans?

9. How would you expect applicants to dress and prepare mentally for an interview?

10. On a more practical matter, how often do you check your email and what alerts and systems can you set up to make sure you notice important messages?

Humility

11. Do you need any special consideration during the application process? (e.g. no language proficiency scores, financial difficulty in sending materials or traveling to the embassy)

12. What can you do on your own to overcome those challenges?

13. Do you communicate well in writing in English?

14. Is there someone you could ask to test your emails to the embassy and university to make sure your message gets across? Preferably, choose someone who is timely, reliable, and not afraid to give you their frank opinion.

15. Are you the kind of person who immediately asks questions or do you do research on your own? If you are tempted to ask questions before doing your own searching, what can you do to help yourself overcome that problem?

Chapter 3: Eligibility

1. What is the last degree you earned? Or, if you are still enrolled in a degree program, what level is that degree and when will you finish all of your graduation requirements? Level: / Completion Date:

2. Have you earned, or will you earn, the prerequisite degree before arriving in Japan (Earned a Bachelor's degree for Master's applicants or a Master's degree for Doctoral applicants)? Yes / No

Your answer to question 2 must be "yes" to be eligible.

3. Do you have Japanese nationality? No / Yes

3.a. If yes, are you a dual national and willing to surrender your Japanese nationality? Yes / No

If you answered "yes" to question 3 and "no" to question 3.a., you are not eligible to apply. Any other combination of answers is eligible.

4. Does your country of nationality have diplomatic relations with Japan? Yes / No

If no, you are not eligible to apply.

5. What year are you applying?

5.a. What year will you start your studies in Japan?

5.b. Subtract 35 from 5.a.

5.c. Is your birth date on or after April 2 of the year you calculated in 5.b.? Yes / No

If you answered "no", and you do not meet the exception requirements described in the age section, you are not eligible.

6. Do you have language proficiency test scores for the language you plan to study in? Yes / No

6.a. If not, and you are not a native speaker, when is the next TOEFL iBT/IELTS/JLPT test in your area?

Reference:

- TOEFL iBT Test Dates and Locations:
  http://www.transenzjapan.com/toefl/
- IELTS Test Dates and Locations:
  http://www.transenzjapan.com/ielts/
- JLPT Test Dates and Locations:
  http://www.transenzjapan.com/jlpt/

7. In what ways could you leverage your research to contribute to the local community (e.g. giving presentations or lessons to community groups, working on specific projects)?

8. Are you willing to get involved in visits to schools and public organizations or volunteer at festivals and events while in Japan? Yes / No

9. Are you currently an active-duty member of the military or a civilian employed by the military? No / Yes

9.a. If you answered yes to question 9, are you able to be discharged or released from your contract before you would start your studies in Japan? Yes / No

You must have answered "no" to question 9 or "yes" to question 9.a. to be eligible.

10. Is there any reason (work, school, inability to obtain passport) that you would be unable to leave your home country during the time specified by MEXT to arrive in Japan? No / Yes

You must have answered "no" to question 10 to be eligible.

11. Have you ever been deported from Japan or left Japan under a Departure Order in the past? No / Yes

11.a. If you answered "yes" to question 11, you will have a

specific period during which you are not permitted to reenter Japan. When does that period end?

11.b. Would your studies start after that date? Yes / No

You must have answered "no" to question 11 *or* "yes" to question 11.b to be eligible.

12. Have you received a MEXT scholarship (other than the Japanese Studies Scholarship, the Japan-Korea Joint Government Scholarship Program For The Students In Science and Engineering Departments, or the Young Leaders Program) in the past? No / Yes

12.a. If you answered "yes" to question 12, what was the last month when you received a scholarship payment?

12.b. How many months of university enrollment or employment as a faculty member or researcher do you have since that date, starting with the month after your last payment?

You must have answered "no" to question 12 or "36" or higher to question 12.b to be eligible.

13. (University Recommendation, only) Do you plan to apply to only one university per year via the University Recommendation process? Yes / No

You must have answered "yes" to question 13.

14. Are you currently enrolled in a university in Japan with a "Student" residence status? No / Yes

14.a. If you answered "yes" to question 14, will you graduate and return to your home country before the start of the degree program that you are applying to via the MEXT scholarship? Yes / No

You must have answered "no" to question 14 or "yes" to question 14.a to be eligible.

15. Do you plan to enroll in a Japanese university as a self-financed student between the time you apply for the MEXT scholarship and when you arrive in Japan to start your scholarship-funded studies? No / Yes

15.a. If you answered "yes" to question 15, can you prove that your program will end and that you will return to your home country at least two months before the start of your scholarship program?

You must have answered "no" to question 15 or "yes" to question 15.a to be eligible.

16. Are you applying for or have you been selected for any other scholarships that will provide money for tuition, living expenses, etc., during your time as a MEXT scholar? No / Yes

If you answered "yes" for question 16, you must be prepared to cancel your application or withdraw from the award for any other scholarships. (But not for grants for specific projects, etc.)

17. Does your research plan require you to conduct field research or participate in an internship outside of Japan? No / Yes

You must have answered "no" to question 17 to be eligible.

18. If you have a Doctoral degree already, are you applying for a Doctoral degree program under the MEXT scholarship? Yes / No

You must have answered "yes" to question 18 to be eligible.

19. Describe how your intended field of study in Japan is directly related to your major or to research you have already conducted at university.

20. Write the name of at least one university in Japan that teaches your field of study at the degree level you want in a language you are qualified to speak. You can find programs

taught in English at any of the sites below:

- JASSO: List of Universities with degrees taught in English: http://www.transenzjapan.com/jasso/
- JPSS: List of Universities with degrees taught in English: http://www.transenzjapan.com/jpss/
- Univ in Japan: Lists of English-Taught Degree Programs: http://www.transenzjapan.com/univ/

21. Do you plan to pursue a professional degree in medicine or dentistry? No / Yes

Unless you are fluent in Japanese (native level), your answer to question 21 must be "no" to be eligible.

22. Does your research concern materials or technology that could conceivably be used for the development or production of weapons of mass destruction? No / Yes

Your answer to question 22 must be "no" to be eligible.

23. Are you currently residing in Japan with a residence status other than "Temporary Visitor"? No / Yes

23.a. If you answered Yes to question 23, prepare an explanation of exactly when and why you plan to leave Japan and surrender your current residence status. One paragraph to half a page should be sufficient.

24. Calculate your GPA using the TranSenz GPA Spreadsheet (or by hand). You can download the spreadsheet from:

http://www.transenzjapan.com/bonusmms1/

What is your GPA (maximum 2 decimal places)?

Your answer to question 24 must be 2.30 or higher.

Chapter 4: Your Application Strategy
Developing Your Goal

1. In what way do you want to serve the world (What is your application theme)?

2. Brainstorm specific things you could do that would contribute to that theme.

3. Narrow down your brainstorm list to goals that you can reasonably accomplish within 5 years that are related to your research background. List your top 3-5 goals, in order of preference.

SMART Goals

4. After reading the section on Relevance, circle the goal from question 3 that you are most passionate about, for your own benefit.

5. In one to two sentences, explain why achieving your goal is important to you personally. What is in it for you?

6. What exact outcome to you plan to achieve?

7. Where will your outcome's area of impact be?

8. When will you achieve this outcome?

9. How will you go about achieving the outcome?

10. Why does this outcome support your application theme?

11. Write a draft sentence that incorporates the answers to question 6 - 10 in a single goal statement.

12. If your goal requires any sequential steps, write out each step and the deadline for that step to ensure that you meet your overall completion deadline.

13. What external support (funding, cooperation,

permission, etc.) does your goal require?

14. For each support you listed in question 132, describe how you plan to secure it, or if it is impossible to secure, write an alternative final goal that will not require that support.

15. What obstacles do you face in your goal? Consider physical, technological, political, and personal obstacles.

16. For each obstacle in question 15, write how you will overcome or avoid it.

17. What specific aspect of your goal will you measure to determine when it is complete (or how close it is to being complete?

18. If you had to modify your end goal because of obstacles or reliance on outside support, rewrite your goal statement with the new final objective.

Why Your Goal Requires Study in Japan

19. How does your goal require additional, original research?

20. If you cannot identify a clear relationship between the need for research and your goal, rewrite your goal statement so that it does require research, knowledge, understanding, or technology that you do not yet have access to but can acquire during your time in Japan.

21. Why does your research have to be conducted in Japan, or at a particular university in Japan?

22. List all of the ways you can think of that your efforts to attain your post graduation goal could strengthen the relationship between your home country and Japan.

23. List any supporting activities related to your goal that you could do to promote connections between your home country and Japan after graduation.

Considering Your Opposition's Needs

24. How can attaining your goal lead to you becoming a leader in your home country, so that you can be an effective cultural ambassador for Japan? Include the field where you plan to become a leader.

25. (Especially if you are applying for the Embassy Recommendation) How does your goal serve your home country?

26. What value does your research plan offer to a potential adviser in Japan?

Your Superpowers

27. What do you do better than most people around you?

28. What do other people come to you for help with?

29. What are you so passionate about that you would do it all day, even if you were not getting paid?

30. When you work in a group, what task to you usually take on?

31. Ask your friends or family what they think you are good at and write those down, too.

32. What are the common underlying abilities that support each of your superpowers?

Leveraging Your Past

33. What academic experiences do you have (high grades, study abroad, research assistantship, publications, presentations, etc.)? List each experience and at least one way that you can connect that experience to your goal for your MEXT scholarship or to one of your superpowers that will give you an advantage over other applicants.

34. List the languages other than Japanese or English

where you have any proficiency and your level (academic, daily conversation, minimal).

34.a. For any academic-level proficiency, how can you use that to serve your research interest in Japan? Are there particular advantages that language offers?

34.b. For daily conversation or minimal proficiency, how can you use that ability to show your adaptability to new cultures and/or willingness to interact?

35. List any professional certifications you have related to your field of study and connect them to your specific research.

36. List any professional certifications you have that are *not* related to your field of study. Is there some way you can leverage them to show your dedication and follow-through ability, which also connecting them to your goal in Japan?

37. What experience do you have with Japanese culture or working with Japanese people? For each one, list the experience as well as one or two ways that having that experience makes you better prepared to adjust to life in Japan.

38. What, if any, disadvantages or obstacles might hold back your application? For each one, list a justification that connects to your goal.

APPENDICES

APPENDIX A: GPA CONVERSION CHARTS

Converting your GPA to MEXT's strange 3.0 system can be the most challenging part of determining whether or not your are eligible - or competitive - for the scholarship.

The conversion process is going to be different based on your country or university's grading system.

Grading System

When I processed MEXT scholarship applications, we would always ask applicants to submit both their grades and an explanation of the grading system. Many applicants were confused by the latter.

A grading system is a chart or list showing all of the possible grades, marks, or scores you could have earned in any given class as well as what the various grades means. The chart should explain which grades are considered to be excellent, good, average, poor, and failing. They do not necessarily need to use those labels, so long as there is a clear stratification.

Whether universities use letter grade or number grades, systems can be very different, even if they use the same letters or numbers, the respective values can differ as we will see in the examples below. That is why you need to show exactly which system applies for your university.

Grading Buckets

A grading bucket is a group of grades that all have the same value. For example, the grades "A+", "A", and "A-" might be considered one grading bucket. Or the a score range of "100 - 80" might be a single grading bucket.

When you convert your grades, you will need to determine how many buckets your system has and which grades correspond to each bucket. Typically, you should have 4 or 5 buckets. Multiple grades may fit into each of those buckets, as we will show in the examples below.

In some cases, you may encounter a system with only three buckets (e.g. distinction, pass, fail), but I have only once encountered something like this and it was at an open university. I will explain that system below as well. For systems with more than 5 apparent buckets, we will squeeze them into 5, using the charts that follow.

There are a few complications you may run into in assigning your grades to different buckets are subgrades or the average marks system.

For subgrades, such as +/- or combined grades like A/B, refer to the grading system, if there is one. If your grading system does not explain the subgrades, you can *probably* ignore the "+" and "-", but if you want a more conservative estimate, treat "-" grades as the next lower bucket.

Note: Grades followed by a 0, such as A0, B0, etc., are not subgrades. Treat them as being the same as an A or B, respectively.

If your university uses the Average Marks System of adding total earned marks and dividing by the total available marks, while not giving specific grades for each class, you still need to convert based on the percentage of marks you earned in each individual class. You would use the same percentages as you do for the overall marks conversion. In that case, multiply each grade by the total number of marks available for the class, instead of credits.

Conversion for Your Reference, Only

I have included charts for specific countries and

universities that I have direct experience with (transcripts or official explanations on university websites that I have physically checked and confirmed as a university employee), but please note that these conversions are based only on my experience and how we did things where I worked. These are not hard and fast rules and may be up to interpretation.

Ultimately, the score that you convert is not going to be your official score. The university or embassy will not accept your math. They will convert it themselves and use their results for processing your application. The point in doing the conversion yourself is just to make sure you are eligible in advance.

GRADING SYSTEMS WITH EXAMPLES AND CONVERSION CHARTS

Here are examples of several different grading systems with conversion charts for each, as well as images of the grading system explanations taken from transcripts from various universities.

The images below come from scans of transcripts or websites that I have used or that past applicants have sent me. The quality may vary as most of these are actual scans. If none of the grading systems below matches yours and you want me to add yours to the examples, please email me a scan or image of your grading system (I do not need to see your actual grades) to travis@transenzjapan.com with the subject line "Grading Scale Check".

Letter Grade Systems

Letter grade systems, typically A through F, are common in many countries, including the US, most of Europe (ECTS), many universities in East and Southeast Asia, and of course, Japan. However, there are several different ways of interpreting the relative value of these grades. Typically, Japanese universities will interpret the grades according to their own understanding, unless you have a grading scale to show them otherwise.

Letter grades can have pluses (e.g. A+), minuses (e.g. A-), zeroes (e.g. A0), or combined letters (e.g. A/B), which complicate the interpretation. I will include as many examples as possible below.

MEXT offers two official examples of how to convert letter grades to its 3.0 scale: A 4-bucket system and a 5-bucket system. I will show some specific examples of each, including variations, on the following pages.

Letter Grades: 4 Letters (ABCF), Official

Grading System (Official): ABCF				
Local Grade	A	B	C	F
MEXT Grade	3	2	1	0
Used in: Example from official MEXT guidelines, Taiwan				

This is the official example from MEXT, but I have only ever seen it used for graduate programs. For graduate programs, a "C" is typically considered the minimum passing grade and expectations are higher in general.

Here is an example of a grading system showing this scale, for graduate school grades.

Systems : UG=Undergraduate : PG=Postgraduate
Grade remark g = Exempt, W = Withdraw, TR = Transfer Credit   Page 1
For Undergraduate, 60 is the passing grade
   80 or More = A {G.P.A 3}; 70 to 79 = B {G.P.A 3}; 60 to 69 = C {G.P.A.2}; 50 to 59 = D {G.P.A 1}; 49 & Below = F {G.P.A 0}
For Graduate 70 is the passing grade
   85 or More= A {G.P.A 4}; 75 to 84 = B {G.P.A.3}; 70 to 74 = C {G.P.A 2}; 69 & Below = F {G.P.A 0}

Of course, citizens of Taiwan are not eligible to apply for the MEXT scholarship, but international students who graduate from Taiwanese universities would be eligible.

Letter Grades: 5 Letters (ABCDF, etc.), Official

MEXT offers two official 5-bucket letter grade conversion scales, but one of these is a system I have never seen in practice:

Grading System (Official): SABCF					
Local Grade	S	A	B	C	F
MEXT Grade	3	3	2	1	0
Used in: Example from official MEXT guidelines					

The one I do see more commonly is:

Grading System (Official): ABCDF					
Local Grade	A	B	C	D	F
MEXT Grade	3	3	2	1	0
Used in: Example from official MEXT guidelines, Taiwan					

Most often, you will see this system with pluses and minuses, as in the examples on the following pages.

Letter Grades: 5 Letters, with Plus/Minus

The rest of the letter grade conversion tables are *not official*. These are based on examples and methods that I have personally used, but in some places they may be up for interpretation.

Five-letter systems with pluses and minuses are, by far, the most common system I see. There are several different variations on the system. Some universities may use only pluses and no minuses. Some may specify a non-plus/minus grade with a zero (such as "A0") to make it impossible to forge into a plus later. Some may use "E" for a failing grade and some may use "F".

I will list all of the most common variants in the table below, but keep in mind that not all of the grades listed in each bucket may apply to you, as you will be able to see from the example images below. That is not a problem.

There are a few important exceptions to this chart, regarding minuses, that we will cover below.

Grading System: ABCDF (with +,-)				
Local Grade	A+, A, A-	B+, B, B-	C+, C, C-	D+, D, D-	E, F
MEXT Grade	3	3	2	1	0
Used in: Brunei, Canada, Hong Kong, Korea, Macau, Malaysia, Singapore, Thailand, USA				

Examples:

Grade	Standard	Grade Point
A+	Excellent	4.0
A		4.0
A-		3.7
B+	Good	3.3
B		3.0
B-		2.7
C+	Satisfactory	2.3
C		2.0
C-		1.7
D+	Pass	1.3
D		1.0
F	Fail	0.0
*P	Ungraded pass	Not included in GPA calculation
*D	Distinction	

* The grades of Distinction and Ungraded pass only apply to some courses

In this example, the descriptions of each grade level makes it very easy to know which grades belong in which bucket. If you have a similar system that shows standards like the example above, use that as your guide to understand how to group your grades.

This example shows what a grading scale would look like with no minuses and no A+. This does not change how grades are sorted using the chart above.

Here's an example showing a university that uses zeroes to designate a neutral grade. In that case, an "A0" would be an "A" in the chart above.

216

Letter Grades: 5 Letters, with Plus/Minus - Variations

I mentioned above that there are some exceptions to the chart above. The most dangerous one is grading systems that specify that a minus grade should be considered to be grouped with the next lower letter grade. As you can imagine, this can have a significant effect on your overall GPA calculation.

Here's what the conversion chart would look like:

Grading System: ABCDF (drop -)					
Local Grade	A+, A	A-, B+, B	B-, C+, C	C-, D+, D	F
MEXT Grade	3	3	2	1	0
Used in: Morocco					

And here's an example of they grading system explanation that would result in the chart above:

A+	4	Excellent
A	4.00	
A-	3.67	Good
B+	3.33	
B	3	
B-	2.67	Fair
C+	2.33	
C	2	
C-	1.67	Pass
D+ *	1.33	
D*	1	
F	U	Fail

It is also possible that only some minuses would be dropped, like the example on the next page, where a C- is dropped to be a failing grade.

Grading System: ABCDF (C- Fail)					
Local Grade	A+	A, A-	B+, B, B-	C+, C	C-, D+, D, F
MEXT Grade	3	3	2	1	0
Used in: Malaysia					

MARKAH / MARKS	GRED / GRADE	MATA GRED / GRADE POINT	MAKSUD / MEANING
90 - 100	A+	4.0	Amat Cemerlang /Excellent
80 - 89	A	4.0	Cemerlang / Distinction
75 - 79	A-	3.7	Cemerlang / Distinction
70 - 74	B+	3.3	Kepujian / Good
65 - 69	B	3.0	Kepujian / Good
60 - 64	B-	2.7	Kepujian / Good
55 - 59	C+	2.3	Lulus / Pass
50 - 54	C	2.0	Lulus / Pass
45 - 49	C-	1.7	Gagal / Fail
40 - 44	D+	1.3	Gagal / Fail
35 - 39	D	1.0	Gagal / Fail
00 - 34	F	0.0	Gagal / Fail

Like the first example I gave of a 5-letter system with pluses and minuses, in a system with clear quality descriptions next to each group of letter grades, so those would take precedence.

Letter Grades: 3 or 4 Letters, with Plus/Minus

While not as common as 5-letter grading systems, you may find some 4-letter grading systems with pluses and minuses, which would be evaluated as below:

Grading System: ABCDEF with Specified Pass Cut-Off			
Local Grade	A+, A, A-	B+, B, B-	C+, C, C-	D, E, F
MEXT Grade	3	2	1	0
Used in: New Zealand, Taiwan			

As you can see in this example, B- is the minimum passing grade for a graduate student. So, if you were converting graduate program grades, than a C+, C, and C- would be grouped in with the failing grades and calculated as zero points. (It would not be possible for a graduate level grade to convert to a "1" in this system.)

Letter Grades: ECTS

ECTS, the common standard in Europe, is a 6-bucket system and, in general grades earned under the ECTS system are harsher than those under the US or Japanese systems. World Education Services (WES), an internationally recognized company that maintains conversion tables from almost all countries' systems to the US 4.0 system, converts an ECTS "C" to an American "B" for GPA purposes (3.0 out of 4).

If you are a European applying via the Embassy Recommendation, you do not need to worry, since all other applicants will have been graded on the same system and the embassy should be familiar with it.

However, if you completed your degree at a European university but are applying for Embassy Recommendation in another country, or you are applying for University Recommendation, the reviewers might not realize that ECTS grades are stricter than other countries' letter grades. In that case, it is in your interest to include an official from your university chart that shows the equivalency between ECTS and US letter grades, for example. Ask your university's study abroad or admissions office if they have something like that you can reference!

Here are two ways to interpret ECTS letter grades. The first is how I would do it, based on my experience working with hundreds of students from across Europe. The second, strict model is how someone who did not understand ECTS might interpret your grades. If you want to be strict on yourself, for the sake of making sure that you meet the eligibility criteria, use the second scale. Remember, your conversion is not official, anyway, so you can not hurt yourself by being harsh.

ECTS Scale 1:

Grading System: ECTS					
Local Grade	A, B	C	D	E	Fx, F
MEXT Grade	3	3	2	1	0
Used in: Europe					

ECTS Scale 2 (Strict):

Grading System: ECTS (Strict)					
Local Grade	A	B	C	D, E	Fx, F
MEXT Grade	3	3	2	1	0
Used in: Europe					

Level	ECTS Grade	Value
Excellent	A	1
Very good	B	1,5
Good	C	2
Satisfactory	D	2,5
Sufficient	E	3
Failed	F	4

The Grading Scale

Danish Grade	Definition	ECTS Grade
12	For an excellent performance displaying a high level of command of all aspects of the relevant material, with no or only a few minor weaknesses.	A
10	For a very good performance displaying a high level of command of most aspects of the relevant material, with only minor weaknesses.	B
7	For a good performance displaying good command of the relevant material but also some weaknesses.	C
4	For a fair performance displaying some command of the relevant material but also some major weaknesses.	D
02	For a performance meeting only the minimum requirements for acceptance.	E
00	For a performance which does not meet the minimum requirements for acceptance.	Fx
-3	For a performance which is unacceptable in all respects.	F

Both grading systems above clearly show that E is a passing grade, so it should be alone as the only 1-point value. The real question is how to treat "C". In these examples, "C" is "Good", as opposed to its meaning of "Average" in the US system. Therefore, it should be considered to be equivalent to a US "B" (also good) and scored at 3 points on the MEXT scale.

Percentage Scales

Like letter grades, the meaning of percentages can vary significantly from country to country. There seem to be two major philosophical outlooks on what the percentage should mean.

In countries like the US and Japan, where you tend to see high grades, the score seems to indicate what percentage of the mastery or performance *expected of a student in the course* you have achieved. In this system, students should be aiming for 100%.

In Europe, the UK, and countries with marks systems, the score seems to indicate instead what percentage of *mastery of the subject* you have achieved. In that case, even the professor might not earn 100% and for a student, earning 70% would be outstanding.

Think about your own system and the normative scores there as you read through the systems and charts below.

Percentage Grades: 4 Ranges, Official

Grading System: Official: Percentage				
Local Grade	100 - 80	79 - 70	69 - 60	59 - 0
MEXT Grade	3	2	1	0
Used in: Example from official MEXT guidelines, Taiwan				

This is one of MEXT's official guidelines for converting percentages. Like the 4-Letter system we discussed at the top, you would primarily see this system used for graduate grades, as in the example below (Note that for undergraduate grades, there are 5 ranges).

Remarks : 100 is the full mark
80 - 100 = A 4   50 - 59 = D 1
70 - 79 = B 3   49 and below = E 0
60 - 69 = C 2   For the graduate students,the passing grade is 70.
W : withdraw   For the undergraduate students,the passing grade is 60.

Percentage Grades: 4 Ranges, Variations

In some universities, you will find grading systems with four percentage ranges, but different cut-offs, as in the examples below. In this case, you would use the cut-off specified in your university's grading system, not the standard table from MEXT, above.

Here is one example from the Philippines:

Grading System: Philippines Percentage				
Local Grade	100 - 92	91 - 83	82 - 75	74 - 0
MEXT Grade	3	2	1	0
Used in: Philippines				

A Excellent, 4 Quality Points (1, 92-100); B+ Very Good, 3.5 Q.P. (1.5, 87-91); B Good, 3 Q.P. (2, 83-86); C+ Satisfactory, 2.5 Q.P. (2.5, 79-82); C Sufficient, 2 Q.P. (3, 75-78); D Passing, 1 Q.P.; I Incomplete, 0 Q.P.; F Failure, 0 Q.P.; WP Withdrawal from course with permission, no Q.P.; W Withdrawal from course without permission, 0 Q.P.; S Satisfactory performance in a remedial course, credit but no quality point; U Unsatisfactory performance in a remedial course, credit but no quality point; AUD Audit, no quality point.

Here is another example from a UK university that uses percentage grades as well as the Honours system that we will discuss below. The UK grading system belongs to the second philosophical outlook, where 70% is an outstanding grade and 100% is essentially impossible for a student to achieve.

Grading System: Honors - Numerical				
Local Grade	69.5% and higher	69.4% - 59.5%	59.4 % - 39.5%	39.4% - 0
MEXT Grade	3	2	1	0
Used in: UK				

Numercial Mark:	Honours Classification:	Non-Honours Classification:
69.5% and over	1 (First Class)	Distinction (where applicable)
59.5-69.4%	2.1 (Upper Second Class)	Merit (where applicable)
49.5-59.4%	2.2 (Lower Second Class)	Pass
39.5-49.4%	3 (Third Class)	
39.4% and lower	Fail	Fail

This degree classification system is in widespread use in the United Kingdom and is believed to represent objective of

In this example, the Non-Honours classification shows four clear buckets and a reviewer would be likely to follow those in assigning scores. Even though a much lower percentage is required to achieve the top range of scores in this system, as anyone can attest, it is at least as difficult to earn a 70% in a UK class as it is to earn a 90% in the US. This system is likely to be brutal on students' grade conversions.

I would argue that a more lenient interpretation is appropriate, but I will discuss that when we return to this example in the "Descriptive Grades" section below.

Percentage Grades: 5 Ranges, Official

MEXT's official standard for converting 5 range percentage scores is based on how percentages are assigned in Japan, where 100% is achievable for students.

Grading System: Official: Percentage					
Local Grade	100 - 90	89 - 80	79 - 70	69 - 60	59 - 0
MEXT Grade	3	3	2	1	0
Used in: Example from official MEXT guidelines, USA, Mongolia, China					

The example I used for the 4-range image above would be a 5-range scale for undergraduates. Here is another example of what that score system might look like.

scores	100-90	89-80	79-70	69-60	≤ 59
grades	Excellent	Good	Average	Pass	Fail

Percentage Grades: 5 Ranges, Variations

Some universities have a more "lenient" percentage scale. Although, as in the example of the UK system above, any apparent leniency in the system is a reflection of how much more difficult it is to earn the corresponding grades.

Grading System: Canada Percentage					
Local Grade	100 - 80	79 - 70	69 - 60	59 - 50	49 - 0
MEXT Grade	3	3	2	1	0
Used in: Canada					

Percentage	Letter Grade	Grade Point Value	Grade Meanings
90-100	A+	4.0	
85-89	A	4.0	Excellent
80-84	A-	3.7	
77-79	B+	3.3	
73-76	B	3.0	Good
70-72	B-	2.7	
67-69	C+	2.3	
63-66	C	2.0	Adequate
60-62	C-	1.7	
57-59	D+	1.3	
53-56	D	1.0	Marginal
50-52	D-	0.7	
0-49	F	0.0	Inadequate

Ignoring the quality of the image, this is a beautifully simple system to interpret.

Descriptive Grades

Some universities skip letters and numbers to describe students' performance directly with words.

Descriptive Grades: 4 Levels, Official

The system below will look familiar to you if you have completed the MEXT scholarship application form, particularly the part where you have to rate your language ability.

Grading System (Official): Description				
Local Grade	優 (Excellent)	良 (Good)	可 (Pass)	不可 (Fail)
MEXT Grade	3	2	1	0
Used in: Example from official MEXT guidelines				

While this is an official conversion scale, I have never seen a university that uses it.

Descriptive Grades: 5 Levels

MEXT does not offer an official conversion scale for 5-level descriptive grades. However, in practice, every descriptive system I have seen had 5 levels. Those systems would be converted just like any other 5-level system.

Descriptive Grades: 5-Level Honours

As I discussed above, I believe all Honours grades should be converted on a 5-level scale, based on my experience. The scale below, from another UK university, shows how this could be done.

Grading System: Honours System (with third)					
Local Grade	First Class	Upper Second	Lower Second	Third	Fail
MEXT Grade	3	3	2	1	0
Used in: UK					

Honours	General	CAS	CGS	US
First Class	Outstanding	20	A1, A2	A+
		19	A3	A
		18	A4, A5	A
Upper second	Very Good	17	B1	A-
		16	B2	B+
		15	B3	B+
Lower second	Good	14	C1	B
		13	C2	B
		12	C3	B-
Third	Pass	11	D1	C+
		10	D2	C
		9	D3	C-
Fail	Marginal Fail	8	E1	D
		7	E2	D
		6	E3	D
	Clear Fail	0-5	F1, F2, F3 G1, G2, G3	F

This system also has several other grading scales, but the important thing is that it shows the description for each level of Honours. This clearly shows that a Lower second is "good" and should be considered in the "B" range of US grades.

Descriptive Grades: Distinction

Another descriptive grading system is the Distinction system used by some universities in Australia and New Zealand. The first time I reviewed a transcript on this system, I was shocked to see that the student had earned all "C" and "D" grades. At first glance, I thought there was no way this student could be eligible, until I saw what those letters meant.

	Grading System: Distinction Marking				
Local Grade	HD (High Distinction), 100 - 80	D (Distinction), 79 - 70	C (Credit), 69 - 60	P (Pass), 59 - 50	N (Fail) 49 - 0
MEXT Grade	3	3	2	1	0
Used in: Australia					

HD   High distinction   80% plus
D   Distinction   70%-79%
C   Credit   60%-69%
P   Pass   50%-59%
UP   Ungraded pass
EP   External institution pass
PC   Pass conceded
N   Fail
XN   Failure, not assessed
NP   Pass following supplementary examination
   (withdrawn from use in 1994)
NN   Failure following supplementary examination
   (withdrawn from use in 1994)
WL   Withdrawn without academic penalty
WN   Withdrawn fail
WR   Withdrawn, debt remission
WRN   Withdrawn, debt remission, academic penalty

Descriptive Grades: 3 Levels

One applicant sent me a copy of a 3-level descriptive grading system. These grades were from an open university, where faculty would not have much time and energy to focus on individual students. Most students simply get a "satisfactory", or passing, grade in each course if they do the work. Unfortunately, since that is the lowest possible passing grade, it gets converted as a 1 on the MEXT scale. This essentially makes it impossible to meet the MEXT eligibility requirements.

If your only degree program is in an open university or other university that similarly does not give much time or care to grading students, you will face significant difficulty in the application. If you are taking an open university degree program alongside a regular university's degree program, then it may actually serve your interests to withdraw from or suspend your open university courses during the application period, so that you do not have to report it as part of your ongoing educational background and a factor in your GPA.

Grading System: 3-Level Descriptive				
Local Grade	Honor	(none)	Satisfactory	Unsatisfactory
MEXT Grade	3	2	1	0
Used in: Open universities				

Educational Evaluation

Grading System

H or H*	=	Honor	76 - 100%	(4.0)
S or S*	=	Satisfactory	60 - 75%	(2.3)
U or U*	=	Unsatisfactory	0 - 59%	(0.0)
*	=	re - examination		

Numerical Grading Scales and GPA

While MEXT's 3.0 GPA system is not actually used anywhere in the world that I am aware of, I have seen a number of other GPA systems or numerical grading scales.

The most common GPA scale is the 4.0 scale. I have also seen 4.3, common in Korea, 4.5 in some universities in Canada, 5.0 in Singapore and many others. However, in each of the examples above, the universities in question also had letter grades or percentage grades listed, so it would be easier to convert the grades using that information.

Numerical: 3-Point Inverted Scale

In this 4-bucket scale, used in some universities in the Philippines, 1 is the highest possible grade and there is actually no numerical mark that corresponds with failure. Since the example below also uses letter grades alongside the numerical grades, failure is indicated by letter, only.

Grading System: Philippines 1-3 system				
Local Grade	1	1.5 - 2	2.5 - 3	(none)
MEXT Grade	3	2	1	0
Used in: Philippines				

A Excellent, 4 Quality Points (1, 92-100); B+ Very Good, 3.5 Q.P. (1.5, 87-91); B Good, 3 Q.P. (2, 83-86); C+ Satisfactory, 2.5 Q.P. (2.5, 79-82); C Sufficient, 2 Q.P. (3, 75-78); D Passing, 1 Q.P.; I Incomplete, 0 Q.P.; F Failure, 0 Q.P.; WP Withdrawal from course with permission, no Q.P.; W Withdrawal from course without permission, 0 Q.P.; S Satisfactory performance in a remedial course, credit but no quality point; U Unsatisfactory performance in a remedial course, credit but no quality point; AUD Audit, no quality point.

Numerical: 4-Point Inverted Scale

While a 4.0 GPA system with 4 being the best score is relatively common around the world, there are some 4-point systems where 1 is the best score, as shown below.

This particular university also uses ECTS scores, but there may be some universities that only show one or the other.

Grading System: 1 (best) - 4 (worst) Scale					
Local Grade	1 - 1,5	2	2,5	3	4
MEXT Grade	3	3	2	1	0
Used in: Czech Republic (also uses ECTS)					

Level	ECTS Grade	Value
Excellent	A	1
Very good	B	1,5
Good	C	2
Satisfactory	D	2,5
Sufficient	E	3
Failed	F	4

Numerical: 5-Point Scale

The Finnish example below uses a 5-point scale but has no numerical grade designated for failure, so all grades shown in numbers will have at least some value.

Grading System: 5-Point Scale					
Local Grade	5	4 - 3	2	1	
MEXT Grade	3	3	2	1	0
Used in: Finland					

Grading Scale:
5 =excellent
4 =very good
3 = good
2 = satisfactory
1 = sufficient
hyv. = passed, no grading
kiit. = passed with distinction

Numerical: Danish "7"-Point Scale

I have heard this scale called a seven-point scale by my colleagues in Denmark, despite the fact that the grades range from a high of 12 to a low of -3. Despite that range, there are only 7 possible grades that can be earned.

If you are in Denmark, then the range of grades may matter for calculating averages, but remember that for MEXT, we never take the average. We always convert grade-by-grade.

Grading System: Danish 7-point Scale					
Local Grade	12 - 10	7	4	2	0 - -3
MEXT Grade	3	3	2	1	0
Used in: Denmark (Also uses ECTS)					

The Grading Scale

Danish Grade	Definition	ECTS Grade
12	For an excellent performance displaying a high level of command of all aspects of the relevant material, with no or only a few minor weaknesses.	A
10	For a very good performance displaying a high level of command of most aspects of the relevant material, with only minor weaknesses.	B
7	For a good performance displaying good command of the relevant material but also some weaknesses.	C
4	For a fair performance displaying some command of the relevant material but also some major weaknesses.	D
02	For a performance meeting only the minimum requirements for acceptance.	E
00	For a performance which does not meet the minimum requirements for acceptance.	Fx
-3	For a performance which is unacceptable in all respects.	F

Numerical/GPA: Vietnamese 10-Point GPA

Vietnamese universities grade on a 10-point GPA scale, though some also use letter grades. Although the system is referred to as a GPA scale, students are actually assigned a grade on the 10-point scale for each class. It is those individual course grades, not the overall average, that must be converted.

Grading System: 10.0 GPA Scale					
Local Grade	10.0 - 8.5	8.4 - 7.0	6.9 - 5.5	5.4 - 4.0	3.9 - 0
MEXT Grade	3	3	2	1	0
Used in: Vietnam					

Notes:
(1) The following are commonly used to convert from ten-point grade to letter grade, A+ 9.0 - 10.0, A 8.5 - 8.9, B+ 8.0 - 8.4, B 7.0 - 7.9, C+ 6.5 - 6.9, C 5.5 - 6.4, D+ 5.0 - 5.4, D 4.0 - 4.9, F Below 4.0
(2) From letter grade to four-point grade: A+ = 4.0, A = 3.7, B+ = 3.5, B = 3.0, C+ = 2.5, C = 2.0, D+ = 1.5, D = 1.0 F = 0.0
(3) Graduation Ranking: 3.60 - 4.00, High Distinction; 3.20 - 3.59, Distinction, 2.50 - 3.19, Credit, 2.00 - 2.49, Pass.
(4) (*), (**), (***) at high credits
(5) The codes marked with letter E in their endings are for courses delivered in English

Numerical: 12-Point Scale

The university in the example below also shows the letter grade conversion, but course grades on the actual transcript may be shown by numerical value, only.

Grading System: Canada 12-point Scale					
Local Grade	12 - 10	9 - 7	6 - 4	3 - 1	0
MEXT Grade	3	3	2	1	0
Used in: Canada					

Note that the conversion above applies only to undergraduate grades from the example below. For graduate grades, a 7 is considered the minimum passing grade, so 12- 10 would be a 3, and 9-7 would be a 2. Everything else would be a zero.

Undergraduate and Qualifying Students

A+	12		B+	9		C+	6		D+	3
A	11		B	8		C	5		D	2
A-	10		B-	7		C-	4		D-	1
									F	0

Faculty of Graduate & Postdoctoral Studies
Master's and Doctoral Students

A+	12		B+	9		F	0
A	11		B	8			
A-	10		B-	7			

Numerical: French 20-Point Scale

Grading in France is particularly severe.

My colleagues there tell me that it is because everyone who passes the high school leaving exam has the right to go to higher education. There is no competition to get in to universities. So, the only way they can reduce their student numbers and get rid of the students who have no particular interest or aptitude is by failing them out. It is a significant achievement just to pass and remain enrolled, and the grading scale below reflects that.

Grading System: French 20-point Scale					
Local Grade	20 - 16	15 - 12	11	10 - 9	8 - 0
MEXT Grade	3	3	2	1	0
Used in: France					

SAMPLE CALCULATIONS

Why You Can't Just Convert Your Final Average

It would be easier, right? But it wouldn't be accurate and you would be wasting your time. If you convert your overall average rather than converting individual courses and taking the average of those scores, you could end up with a number that is wildly inaccurate.

For the sake of this example, let's look at two hypothetical students. Both students took 10 total courses and come from a 5-bucket system based on percentage grades, as follows:

Local Grade	Converted Grade
100 - 90	3
89 - 80	3
79 - 70	2
69 - 60	1
59 - 0	0

OK Here are our students' grades:

Course	Student 1	Student 2
	Local Grade	**Local Grade**
Course 1	100	81
Course 2	59	60
Course 3	79	80
Course 4	100	80
Course 5	79	80
Course 6	79	80
Course 7	79	80
Course 8	79	80
Course 9	79	80
Course 10	79	80
Average:	81.2	78.1

Apparently, student 1 did better than student 2. Student 1's final average of 81.2% would convert to a "3" on the MEXT Scale, based on the chart above, while student 2's 78.1% would convert to a 2, and would not be eligible to apply for the scholarship.

Now, let's look at what happens if we convert the grades correctly, one-by-one, with the same two students.

Course	Student 1		Student 2	
	Local Grade	MEXT Converted Grade	Local Grade	MEXT Converted Grade
Course 1	100	3	81	3
Course 2	59	0	60	1
Course 3	79	2	80	3
Course 4	100	3	80	3
Course 5	79	2	80	3
Course 6	79	2	80	3
Course 7	79	2	80	3
Course 8	79	2	80	3
Course 9	79	2	80	3
Course 10<	79	2	80	3
Average: Converted		2		2.8

Now, student 2 has the higher grade, 2.8 overall, which is both eligible and competitive. Student 1, on the other hand, is not even eligible to apply.

If you look again at the grades above, you will see that the difference between the students is that Student 1 earned the highest possible grades in each bucket, while student 2 earned the lowest grades in each bucket. Being on the high end, helped student 1 to have a higher overall average, but when you convert to the MEXT scale, there is no difference between a 100 in this example and an 80. So all that extra credit might have paid off anywhere else, but not for MEXT.

Now, of course I'm not suggesting that you should settle for the lowest grade in each grade bucket and not try harder, I'm just trying to point out why you have to be careful in converting your grade

APPENDIX B: PRIORITY COUNTRIES

For the University Recommendation, at least 75% of universities' nominees in each scholarship category must come from the list below. (An exception is possible for some PGP programs).

The regions in the table below are from the official list on JASSO's website, but the translations are mine.

Africa		
Algeria	Angola	Benin
Botswana	Burkina Faso	Burundi
Cabo Verde	Cameroon	Central African Republic
Chad	Comoros	Cote D'Ivoire
Democratic Republic of the Congo	Djibouti	Egypt
Equatorial Guinea	Eritria	Ethiopia
Gabon	Gambia	Ghana
Guinea	Guinea-Bissau	Kenya
Lesotho	Liberia	Libya
Madagascar	Malawi	Mali
Mauritania	Mauritas	Morocco
Mozambique	Namibia	Niger
Nigeria	Republic of the Congo	Rwanda
Sao Tome and Principe	Senegal	Seychelles

Africa (continued)		
Sierra Leone	Somalia	South Africa
South Sudan	Sudan	Swaziland (eSwatini)
Tanzania	Togo	Tunisia
Uganda	Zambia	Zimbabwe
Americas		
Argentina	Bolivia	Brazil
Chile	Colombia	Ecuador
Guyana	Paraguay	Peru
Suriname	Uruguay	USA
Venezuela		
Asia		
Bangladesh	Bhutan	Brunei
Cambodia	India	Indonesia
Laos	Malaysia	Maldives
Mongolia	Myanmar	Nepal
Pakistan	Philippines	Singapore
Sri Lanka	Thailand	Vietnam
CIS and Russia		
Armenia	Azerbaijan	Belarus
Kazakhstan	Kyrgyzstan	Moldova
Russia	Tajikistan	Turkmenistan
Uzbekistan		
Europe		
Albania	Austria	Bosnia and Herzegovina
Bulgaria	Croatia	Cyprus

Europe (continued)		
Czech Republic	Greece	Hungary
Kosovo	Liechtenstein	Macedonia
Montenegro	Poland	Romania
Serbia	Slovakia	Slovenia
Switzerland	Ukraine	
Middle East		
Afghanistan	Bahrain	Iran
Iraq	Israel	Jordan
Kuwait	Lebanon	Oman
Palestine	Qatar	Saudi Arabia
Syria	Turkey	UAE
Yemen		

You can find the original list in Japanese at
http://www.transenzjapan.com/priority/

There are several notable countries not on that list, including (but not limited to): China, South Korea, all of North and Central America (except the US), all of Oceania, all of Scandinavia, and Western Europe, including the UK.

Students from China and South Korea make up nearly 48% of all international students in Japan, but those countries are not on the list. So if you are from either of those two countries or from another country not listed above, you will be facing an uphill battle to get a slot.

APPENDIX C: REFERENCES AND RESOURCES

TranSenz Resources

Bonus Document Pack including the TranSenz GPA Spreadsheet

http://www.transenzjapan.com/bonusmms1/

Mastering the MEXT Scholarship: The Complete Series

http://www.transenzjapan.com/blog/mastering-the-mext-scholarship/

TranSenz Blog: Home to dozens of articles about the MEXT scholarship and the best place for questions and answers.

http://www.transenzjapan.com/blog/

Official MEXT and Japanese Government Resources

List of Japanese Embassies and Consulates Japanese Ministry of Foreign Affairs (English)

http://www.transenzjapan.com/embassies/

Past Embassy Language Proficiency and Other Tests

http://www.transenzjapan.com/tests/

MEXT's Official Scholarship Webpage (Japanese)
Home to all official scholarship application guidelines, forms, and scholarship outline.

http://www.transenzjapan.com/officialmext/

Priority Graduate Programs (PGP) for 2017 (pdf)

http://www.transenzjapan.com/pgp2017/

JASSO's Annual Report on Number of International Students in Japan (Japanese)

http://www.transenzjapan.com/jassostats1/

http://www.transenzjapan.com/jassostats2/

Mext Priority Countries List for 2018 (pdf)

http://www.transenzjapan.com/priority/

Other Resources

VisualPing

VisualPing is a free tool for tracking changes to specific areas of websites, such as the MEXT page that shows the active scholarship applications. You can set a particular area of a site to review on a daily basis and Visual Ping will tell you if there are any changes to that section. I use this tool to let me know when the MEXT official website has released new guidelines.

http://www.transenzjapan.com/ping/

Japan Reference Forum

http://www.transenzjapan.com/jref/

How to Win Friends and Influence People

Perhaps the best book available on how to persuade others to your point of view in a completely genuine way. This is a universal book link that will let you choose the online retailer of your choice, or you can just search for it at your favorite online or brick and mortar book store!

http://www.transenzjapan.com/wfip/